A BROKEN THAT'S UNSPOKEN

Delivered, Healed, and Set Free

A BROKEN THAT'S UNSPOKEN

Delivered, Healed, and Set Free

Skyye Howze

ISBN-13: 978-1548043216
ISBN-10: 1548043214

For information on the content of this book, email
skyyehowze@yahoo.com

WrightStuf Consulting LLC

Columbia, SC
www.wrightstuf.com

Printed in the United States of America

This book is dedicated to women - young and old, married and single - to inspire, motivate, and help them draw closer to God.

Prelude

I harbored those distinct insecurities of loving hard or not wanting to love at all. At times, I wavered in my faith, prayed when I wanted to, and doubted God, trying to fix it on my own. The tears I cried and the pain I held onto deep inside, drained and depressed me, but more so damaged me in areas I couldn't imagine. I harbored secrets I didn't or (couldn't) spill until I got to know God, and the nakedness of my life began to unfold. Yet, in the midst of everything, God kept me. And in my heart, I believed, I surrendered, and by His mercy and grace, I held on.

Then there were the two hearts growing inside of me during my most difficult and trying moments. My "Beautiful Blessing" (Zion) and my "Supernatural Miracle" (Jabari) changed my life and gave me hope and the motivation I needed to continue living. I can smile because they are the reasons I made it.

Today, I am willing to share my story with you because I want you to be healed and touched by my words. I think if I share my journey, you will recognize your own strength and weaknesses of having "A Broken That's Unspoken."

I pray that the wisdom and knowledge I gained can be passed on to you. Just as God delivered, healed, and set me free, I will show you how God's grace can help you survive during your broken moments. If you fall short in any areas of your life, remember that God has not forgotten about you. In fact, He has been with you all the time. It's okay! You don't have to be afraid, have doubts, feel worthless, or unimportant. You are not alone. As you travel on this journey with me, understand that you are fearfully and wonderfully made. God loves you and so do I. YOUR DELIVERANCE BEGINS NOW!

Growing Up Lost

Growing up, I didn't get to experience the fullness of childhood. I had to mature or learn to take care of myself, physically and emotionally, at a very young age. Soon the difficulties of life began to take its toll on me. I started hearing stories about my mother, and I tried not to believe or even listen. I was always in denial about the lifestyle she lived, but when you're a child words stick with you; engraved on your heart. I endured a lot of hurt and pain just to know that the woman who had birthed me in the world had left me to be *in the world*. It takes a mother's heart to love her child and I didn't feel secure or protected - more like abandoned. Even when I didn't understand, I knew God had his unchanging hands around me. He had created a man that loved me too much to let me go.

Although I was a motherless and fatherless child, I had hoped that my loving Father (God) in Heaven would restore me. I had to go through another birthing process to begin to find out who I was. My misery produced sadness, brokenness, and loneliness. There was no possible way I could have enjoyed my childhood after finding out such heartbreaking facts about my parents.

My beloved grandmother (RIP) took me under her wings to nurture me and took on the honorable responsibility of "MOM". Living under her teachings, rules, and strict ways kept me in line many days. If it wasn't for her, I probably wouldn't be the woman that I am today. I was lost, left in the dark, as secrets floated around without my understanding. Somehow, by instinct, I managed to ask hard questions. The first few times frustrated me because there were no clear answers. Finally, the explanation of what my mom and dad did came down on me like a ton of bricks. Just to hear about it crushed me. The way it was revealed to me hurt more than the truth itself.

The truth does hurt but it also helps and heals. It was harsh but that's what I needed to know in order to move forward and away from my brokenness. I'd been steady digging, completely lost. I couldn't understand why my mom left me and at the same time, not having a clue as to who my father was. That fact left my soul damaged and a face full of tears. The closure was everything I needed but not what I wanted. I wasn't ready to handle the pain that came along with my brokenness.

From time to time, we all lose things yet some things we aren't always able to recover. It's hard trying to bounce back but eventually you will be restored and get where you need to be in life.

In my childhood misery, I always knew that God never left my side. Though now my life is everything I need to excel, I had to grow up and be mature quickly. Growing up in my grandmother's house was truly a "home" to me and many others. She welcomed you with hospitality and plenty to eat. I didn't want for anything and I was indeed spoiled with *things*. BUT! Somehow, I lacked security and love, and I felt like an outcast (*The Black Sheep of the Family*). So much went unnoticed with me. I was overlooked intentionally (I thought) in areas that caused me to be broken and bitter. What I needed most I didn't get. You don't know how that saddened me.

Still, I had been the one with the positive outlook on life. Even in negative situations. I never talked about what I would do. I'd move in silence instead. I allowed the passion to burn in my heart, praying to God, exercising the faith. I knew someday I wouldn't struggle anymore.

> *God love the lost and He loves to help us find our way, showing us who we are really created to be on this earth.*

When I was lost, I consumed a lot of hatred, anger, and was not forgiving towards my parents. Sometimes I found myself thinking how my life would have really turned out if I had known my mother and father. Would I have tried to find my own way? Would I have waited to have sex? Would I have made bad choices along with bad habits? My mind pondered on questions that had no answers. At that point, I knew God had to step in to take complete control. I was slowly going insane trying to understand what I couldn't seem to understand. I had to get out of that mindset and focus. Time waits on no one. Life kept moving and so did I.

School was always an escape for me. It gave me hope. It made me dream BIG! I was up for grabs, reaching, trying to learn every new thing. Most kids, even today, would be excited about the latest shoes, brand-name clothing, money, cell phones, and other material things. I was excited just to be educated, to gain wisdom, to gain knowledge, to grow, to expand; just knowing I was working my way up to the top had me joyful inside. My aim was determination *to be somebody.*

While in school, I *pretended*, with a sincere smile. My smile covered up my bitterness, my sadness, and my anger issues that slowly developed over time. I was torn and no one knew a thing. They figured life was good for me. Have you ever heard that saying: "FAKE IT UNTIL YOU MAKE IT"? That's exactly what I was doing. I'm here to tell you my life was far from good. Nowhere near perfect, my soul was in danger.

I recall, as a child, one of my teachers telling me if I just keep God first, keep dreaming, I can have whatever it is I want in life. That stuck with me. It's funny how others see more in you than you see in yourself. This teacher's words pushed me to perform to my highest potential. The teacher believed in me when I didn't believe in myself. Those words breathed life into me. Until then, I didn't have any support or encouragement. What I had was lack of communication and lack of attention. I was helped in that present moment.

Sometimes, not having help really makes you draw closer to God. When family seems distant, God is right there with an "Open Door Policy" ready to provide everything you once lacked. He will offer Love, Support, and Encouragement, giving you the strength to make it. You can always depend on Him when you can't depend on anyone else.

As I moved to the next levels in school, I made progress and good grades. I graduated. NOW I'M A FRESHMAN, elated to be in high school. As I stated previously, I made school an escape for me. I would temporarily forget about the problems of life and dive deep into my studies. Some people let their anger and frustration out through working out at a gym, punching a wall, or the norm, taking it out on a loved one. I would do so with my schoolwork. It eased my pain, it kept me calm, it gave me hope that I wouldn't be in this situation forever. Things will soon change, and my life will be better.

Doing something educational and productive brought my stress level all the way down. My focus was not on the problem but on the solution to get ahead so I wouldn't have a reason to look back. But through it all, keeping God first, prayers and school, was my answer to most things. That's how I got by. (His grace was always sufficient for me).

I'm such an excited person. Most anything gets me hyped. I was eager to learn new things especially meeting new people. Now that was a very big interest for me since *I'm such a Social Butterfly.* I was free flying around enjoying school, my classmates, and the new environment that I had encountered. On the other hand, I wanted to occupy my time with something else besides school itself. I love to laugh, I'm always smiling, and I have an uplifting spirit *(full of life)* so

I tried out for the high school cheerleading team. I MADE IT! My personality fit perfectly.

> *Keep cheering yourself on, rooting being your #1 fan and you will make it too. In fact, you already made it. Believe it and receive it.*

Somehow, I started slacking in my grades, getting in trouble, being influenced; hanging with the wrong crowd; and the biggest distraction of all... BOYS! (*My weakness*). And to make matters worse, I had a boyfriend. I wasn't getting the attention at home, so I took in everything that made me feel loved, even if I had to lust after it. Everything I was tuned into hindered me in so many areas of my life. Things really started to turn out for the worse, but I still found a reason to smile; something I did oh so well. My smile always kept the tears from flowing.

> *Just because things don't go your way, you still can choose to be happy, the sun will soon shine. Don't focus on the rainy days but keep your eyes on God! That's where your real peace begins.*

Soon, I realize why things were falling apart in my life. I left the most important person out of everything. He was the head of my life. My "Spiritual Being" God! He didn't deserve what I did to Him and the amazing person He is, He still loved me, He forgave me and gave me HOPE, MERCY, and GRACE to continue to live. I couldn't bear it any longer. I grew tired of putting my God on the backburner, so I went back to excelling in school.

NOW I'M A SOPHMORE, moving up higher and higher, excelling, and doing great. My favorite season came. I love the summer and school was out. I wasn't too excited though. My summer wasn't much fun. In fact, it was downright boring. Nothing exciting or worthwhile to do, no vacations; I practically stayed in the house. I was most definitely a homebody. Over the summer, I thought about a lot of things concerning my life. I knew I couldn't make it on my own. I had to let God lead me in every aspect of it to cope and stay sane. The emotional pain seemed unbearable. I felt like I had no reason to live. I asked myself time and again, why am I here? Soon those thoughts begin to fade away.

You may be distracted, get off course. The test is never easy. Sometimes you pass or fail, but no matter what it looks like, you must know you are going to succeed to the next level.

Those summer months went by fast and I was back in school. The new school year always started in my birthday month. My birthday is the 7th! The eighth month. August! How excited is that? I was overcome with joy because the number '8' means "new beginnings". The time had come for me to set aside old ways and become a new creature in Christ. I was baptized four days before my 16th birthday. I felt like a new young woman ready to walk in a new season and do things in a new way.

The journey of being a "Church girl" wasn't so cool to me these days. I always loved God, and you might think I'm a fool for saying such, but I always had it in my heart that God would wait for me. I was very ignorant, foolishness at its best. Shame on me! Trying to be ahead of God but all the

7

time, I lived beneath Him. Now I'm sure God would have waited for me as long as I did my part first, then he'd do His! That's how it normally goes, right? Silly me! Although, I still attended Church, what led me into the trouble was my weakness - *I loved boys*!

So you see, it's never about what you done in your past. Sure, you will think about it, but never return to it. Keep moving ahead! The future is what matters most.

I was bold. I put my relationship before God. Obviously, I had my priorities unchecked, and nowhere near decency and order. I stopped going to Sunday school and bible study. I would go to Church service every now and then. Things were so *out of order*, soon I stopped going completely. The devil had me right where he wanted me; not in God's presence. I was so high off love (or shall I say lust), I didn't care about anything. I did what I wanted, and you can bet I reaped everything I sowed, not realizing that GOD'S LOVE IS WAY BIGGER THEN ANY HUMAN'S LOVE.

Now don't get me wrong, it's cool to have someone to date. But make sure the two of you are "equally yoked". Unbelievers and believers don't work well together. Just like oil and water don't mix, the destructiveness that comes along with unequally yoked people is way more than you can handle. Do it God's way. It's the best way.

Suddenly, my mind was made up. From all the distractions, I found it necessary to change schools. A new year; a new environment, a better school system, a new way of learning. I'M A JUNIOR. A totally complete change. I didn't know what to expect but because I love change, I was looking forward to a great school year. Hoping for the best, to be who I needed to be; working hard and paving a way to a new path in my life.

The school year was very laid back but demanding at times. I found that sometimes it could be uncomfortable starting fresh. My new peers said I was anti-social or to use the famous word, "stuck up". Some say that comes with being attractive. They even went on to say some people couldn't stand to look at you. But they never knew me or took the time to get to know who I was deep down inside. Instead, they judged me by my looks, not my character. It was very difficult for me to understand. But being the strong person that I am, I was able to shake it off. I had no other choice but to get over it. I knew who I was. I stayed true to myself, even when others had false things to say.

> We go through a transitioning in life with bumpy roads. But if we keep moving in faith, eventually the road smooths out. You will be the changed person you need to be for God, yourself, and others.

When I transferred schools, I had so many doubts and fears of what would take place. How would this affect me, not only mentally but also physically and spiritually? Then I remembered I was a child to the Most High God who sits high and looks low. I know angels camped around me, protected, and shielded me from harm's way. I became very relaxed and comfortable as restoration began to revive me, refresh me and replenished me. God was a *"spiritual friend"* when I didn't have any natural friends to count on. He helped me cope through life to get the understanding I needed for tough times. I'm so grateful and thankful for the faithfulness.

AT LAST, I'M A SENIOR, transitioning into an amazing woman. I was nearing the end of the race, but it was very nerve-racking and full of excitement at the same time. Knowing that I'm about to enter another phase of my life kept me on the edge with mixed emotions.

> *In life, you will go through "things", but remember, trouble don't last always. The people who once judged you, may come to you for help. Continue to humble yourself and let God use you in a mighty way. Remember, God is the only one who matters.*

As a senior, I learned responsibility, growth, courage, and strength. I remember taking all the state exams to graduate. It was a requirement, and I did what was necessary so I could walk across that stage with dignity and pride; head held high, too. However, I had to take one test again; it was math. That subject was never my strong suit. It kept me frustrated. In fact, I hated math with a passion, but I knew what I needed to do to tackle that situation. I was desperate and determined to get my diploma. I didn't give up, I didn't quit, but I kept praying and pushing until I got through. The third time – PASS.

<u>THE BIG DAY! I GRADUATED.</u> My graduation day, May 14, 2009! On a Thursday to be exact. I stayed up all night, so anxious but fearful too. I was unhappy. I had my family there but what saddened me the most, I couldn't find my mom in the crowd. I didn't just want her to be there I needed her to be there. To see what I'd overcame and accomplished. Not to mention, I still didn't know my dad, so I was down. I didn't want to ruin such a special day for family, my friends, and myself so I cheered up. When the principal called my name within the long line of graduates, I felt so proud because it was such a blessing.

Although, I hadn't received much support and encouragement throughout the school year from my family, they still rooted for me. The best part of my graduation came when the ceremony was over. My mom was there after all. With open arms, she gave me the best kiss, and told me how proud she was of me. Now that day was full of LOVE! It doesn't stop here. If you feel a warm chill in your spirit, you are being delivered as my words stimulate your heart and soul.

In life, you will go through hardships; things that you must face. It may not seem fair or be easy, but I tell you the reward at the end is worth every failed moment, every difficult time. When you accomplish the task, then you will be able to move forward. Don't stop! Keep striving!

Unfinished Business

In my last year of high school, the senior class worked on our "senior book". A big percentage of our grade would come from writing about what we planned to do after graduation. The title was "Where I've been, Where I'm Headed." I will share a part of this writing that I was certain would come to pass.

> ...Walking across the stage is the best day of my life. I succeeded and worked extremely hard like I was supposed to. That's how I got to the exciting part of my life. However, it's time to get into preparation for college, get a career that I'm happy with, and of course, one that I love and have a passion for. I have to attend college four years to get my bachelor's degree and two years to get a master's degree that I will accomplish in 2014...

Four months after graduating from high school, I was a college student at Coahoma Community College in Clarksdale, Mississippi majoring in social work. After weighing my options of three career fields, I finally decided and chose something that my heart burned for...my passion...Social Work.

Whatever it is you are going to school for, never ever give up. Things won't always go as planned, but no matter how many obstacles you face in life keep going. Your passion is what drives you to be a better you for you and your children and your career. Do what you love, and love what you do.

At the beginning of my freshman year of college, I was an off-campus student. At the time, I didn't have transportation, so I got up every day at 5 AM to catch the bus. Boy that was a headache with irritation and much frustration. Not only did I have to get up early in the morning, I had to stay late, waiting until 3 PM to make it home at six that evening. I didn't know which one was worse, but I survived. I had to endure a lot of inconveniences, just to get my education but I had no other choice but to maintain. I knew I needed this to provide a better life for myself. My hard work had to count for something. I made the necessary adjustments to get to where I was going but still felt stuck along the way.

Things don't always go as you would want them to go. You must keep pressing and know God is going to see you through. No matter how tough it seems, your break through is surely on the way.

13

But don't break on the way, instead pray it gets greater later.

I learned the value of a dollar (independence that is) while attending college and working. I never knew how stressful it was to do both until a nervous breakdown was just around the corner. My health was very important, so I had to let my job go and strictly focus on school. I tried to come up with some type of solution because I couldn't afford to go without a job. I didn't want to be without income. Figuring out ways to make ends meet, I asked myself, how would I pay for personal needs? How will I pay for food? How will I pay for school supplies? It was just too much. It overwhelmed my mind. Nevertheless, God still made a way for me. Things were so outrageous at home; family matters; family affairs; family problems every which way. You name it, it was happening. I don't even understand how I kept it all together while focusing on my studies to finish school. Then I had an epiphany that the God I serve never left my side. He was there all the time helping me overcome those obstacles. Even during my storm, somehow, I broke through.

I was a few classes away from graduating with an associate degree in Social Work. I didn't make it. I was so discouraged. I was so close to obtaining my degree, but what I was facing caused me to drop everything to make things easier on my end. After all the pondering I did, I decided to transfer to Delta State University to be close to home. I knew if I couldn't get a ride, I could walk to school because school was a "desire of my heart". I always believed in finishing what I started. No matter how long it took, I would get there eventually with God's help.

When things didn't go as I thought they should, I felt like a loser, a failure, just a *nobody*. I thought it was bad enough that I didn't have support. That really caused me to be depressed - beating myself up mentally, and making me want to give up, not only on school but on life as well. The summer of 2011, I started my second summer session at DSU! I applied for the Social Work Program. I WAS ACCEPTED :) From there, I was on my way.

This was a fresh new start for me so I was excited, ready to explore new ways of learning and new ways of preparing myself for the real world. After finishing up summer school, I decided to stay on campus in the fall. I know you are thinking *why would you stay on campus and you are right in town?* True, but I was too spoiled for my own good. I needed to grow up, to explore. I needed to learn responsibility. I wanted to learn to do things on my own so this fresh start was everything I needed to give me the boost to step up in life.

I didn't do well with people I didn't know so my best friend Casey and I shared a dorm room. I thought that was pretty cool. Plus, we had a passion for the same thing - we wanted to be "social workers". We always talked about making a difference in the world, and what we would do once we graduated; once we obtained our degree in what we loved to do. It was amazing to share these moments with someone I loved dearly.

> *If there is something you want bad enough, chase it. God will help you chase it. Keep Him first and acknowledge Him in all you do, then you will see your blessings flow.*

August 22 was the move-in date for us. Moving was downright tiresome but it had to be done. We did have some help. The football team helped us because they were required to help. I didn't care how tired I was, I was just overjoyed to be in a new environment and see new scenery other than my home. It felt so good to be out on my own. The highlight of my day was meeting new people, seeing new faces, and sparking up random conversations. That's how much of a social butterfly I was.

Moving in different direction and making new friends was so awesome. As I became used to dorm life, a lot of interesting things begin to take place with me. Although, my mind was on socializing, I never lost focus on my studies. I did, however, lose focus on God. I put God all the way back. You would have thought that I would have kept it all together, but the minute I moved on campus the devil moved in with me. I had just recently joined a Church and was on fire for God. All that went out the window.

> *Moving forward to new beginnings to only end up being lost, confused, and misled by the choices that you made causes results in moving backwards, repeating the cycle of the same thing. When you move, move with no distractions.*

And to add on to that distraction I met this guy name Asher. I was headed from night class when he spoke to me. Of course, I spoke back. We stared and smiled at each other. It was for sure love at first sight. We exchanged numbers and went on our way. Although I was seeing someone else, I didn't let that stop me from seeing him too. I didn't rush the process I was going with the flow. It didn't stop me at all from spending time with him. We became best friends. I was falling for this guy and the feeling was mutual. The closer we got the more love showed through our actions. I remember us saying we loved each other at the same time.

My heart burst with joy. He didn't know how much happiness he brought to my life, and I couldn't wait to get over to his dorm room to experience our first encounter. I was curious from the first time he spoke to me. I wanted to know what he was like in bed so badly. Not that it was a factor, but I wondered and wanted to show him just how much I loved him too. I was ready to see what he could do and how he would do it. Funny thing, I was supposed to be practicing celibacy. That didn't last long. I broke that vow the minute I got to his dorm room.

We made love for more than three hours. I didn't expect us to have sex that long. Even though we were sinning and very much wrong, every moment was pleasurable and full of passion. If I wasn't crazy in the head before, after all that lovemaking…I was very much head-over-hills crazy for this guy…in the midst of falling in love and loving him so hard.

After that night, I was drinking alcohol again, having more sex with Asher, listening to secular music, and using foul language. I truly got lost in the lustful desires of the world, doing ungodly things to please my flesh. I knew God wasn't pleased. I did what I wanted to do and damaged my life as a Christian. I risked living for God to be a wild college student. I was just that, but perhaps undercover.

Not only was I deceiving God, I was misleading everyone. I was an innocent college student by day and by night a promiscuous young woman. In my mind, I was doing whatever I needed to do to make ends meet, to survive. Sometimes I didn't have to have sex but could talk a good game. "Conversation rule the nation" so they say. Well on my end, I was doing a lot of ruling. My mouth was very persuasive. I could talk you out of anything. Now everything I was doing was extremely dangerous. My life, in fact, was put on the line because of the foolish moves I was making on my behalf. I could have been killed, BUT GOD! He had his hands wrapped around me even when I strayed away. He protected me from harm's way.

> *Even as a sinner, God will still love you and have mercy on your soul. It doesn't give you the right to do wrong nor continue to sin; but to learn from your mistakes and your ways so you can be right and stay right.*

I was thinking about quitting school. I mean after all, what did I have to lose? I was drowning in my sins so it wouldn't have hurt if I had given up on everything my heart desired. It didn't matter anyway. I was worthless and very unimportant, just going through the motions of life. As life began to roll on by, I was getting deeper into the semester. On top of all that, life's problems began to burden me. Depression set in on me heavy, stress instantly took over my body, and I just wanted to die. I even asked the Lord to take me. I was tired, but I managed, studied hard, stayed focused, did what was mandated, and to my surprise, I pass all my classes. I was proud of how I pulled that off.

In the midst of all I was facing in that particular season of my life, I began to see how clever I was. Behind all the chaos, I was still able to smile. I wasn't happy about the choices that I made at all. My life was tumbling to and from. I'm sure God needed me, but I wasn't available. I was too busy playing devil's advocate, doing things the quick way, merely the wrong way, to only get it all snatched back from me in a matter of seconds.

> *The devil will lure you in to something that will have you happy just for that moment, but he never gets you prepared for the lifetime pain of heartaches, hurt, tears and brokenness that comes along with it. Stay focused. The devil wants to steal your purpose but guard it with your whole life. God needs it to use for his plan he has for your future.*

The year 2011 was such a rollercoaster ride for me. Everything was coming to an end. I was half way through the semester and my favorite break was soon to start. Christmas, even though my family didn't get along well, the laughs, the memories, and the talks was just what I needed to lift my spirit up. And to top that off was my grandmother's cooking. She always cooked with love, made you feel welcomed, loved, and at home. "Home is where the Heart is" and she put every inch of her heart into making Christmas feel like Christmas.

The new year was slowly approaching so I decided ahead of time that I was bringing 2012 in at church; trying to do what's right because my life had fallen apart. I needed Jesus and everything that came with Him. The devil had my soul wrapped up in his hands. I was sinning in ways I never before imagined.

If you strayed away from God, it's okay. He will get your attention one way or another. He will soon lead you back to Christ at your most broken moments. To repair you to be more Christ-like; more like Him, and less of yourself.

At Church service that New Year's Eve night, I remember getting prayer and it was said that *I would be back in Church and the next time I'd come to rededicate my life to Christ. I would stay on the tasks I needed to do on the mission for God.* Did I take heed? I heard but I wasn't listening. It went in one ear and out the other. The devil had me so sewed up. I was always thinking someone was out to get me. I just didn't have the patience for anything or anyone, not even God, which was bad on my end. The devil had me believing that no one could be trusted. I was being used and it tore my life apart. Instead of taking in what was prophesied to me, I was tuned in to the devil's tactics trying to figure my next move.

Never turn a deaf ear to God. He will punish you in ways you will think you are dying. It doesn't feel good. Listen to His word. It helps, it heals, it saves, and it is powerful. It will clean your life up if you obey.

While Asher and I were on bad terms, we weren't sure if we would get back together. There was so much going on and we wanted to stay focused on our studies. We still loved one another the same but chose to continue our relationship as friends. My heart hurt terribly as I was carrying his child. He knew nothing about it for that matter. No one knew. I didn't see my menstrual cycle because the stress was taking over my body; at least that's what I told him. But all in all, I was expecting his baby. I had so many other issues, trying to focus on school and trying to fight for our relationship. I was convinced in my heart and mind that Asher was the one for me. Then a death comes to my family.

The moment I called him, I wanted to tell him so badly that I was pregnant. But to cover all that up, I just mentioned about my grandfather passing. He came over immediately without hesitation; loving on me, caring for me, consoling me. He made sure I ate and got plenty of rest. I cried myself to sleep in his arm because I always felt secured and protected anytime I was with him. He really comforted me in my time of need. Even though we had decided to go our separate ways, it was clear that our hearts were not ready to let go. So, we agreed to continue to have sex just to stay connected. We both knew that it was harmful and unhealthy, but we were willing to risk it. Love had me blind and my heart was tuned into his beat. I was always rocking with him no matter what it looked like.

As bad as it hurt me, I gave the dorm life a rest. My grandmother needed me at home. She was going through a terrible time with the loss of our grandfather. I had to be there and although I didn't want to. We had our differences and did not get along, but I put all that behind me as she went through her grieving process. On top of that, I lost my baby. I wasn't pregnant for too long. My body couldn't handle the stress. My grandmother and I both grieved our losses. While I kept it together in silence, she grieved loudly.

The transition from the *dorm life* to *back at home* depressed me somewhat. It almost seemed like I was going backwards, yet I had to make the decision to be an off-campus student once again. A new school term began and I was a senior; expecting to graduate May of 2013.

Even though, I had worked diligently on my schoolwork, it was time to work extremely hard to get across the stage. Not saying that school wasn't my focus, but I also had my eyes on something else. The Kappa Alpha Psi fraternity, also known as the NUPES, hosted the Kappa Ball that I refused to miss. My best friend, Casey, and I linked up like we always did just to have a great time; wanting to enjoy the moment and, of course, the night. I was on a mission, peeping trying to see whose man I was taking home with me so I could get laid. I didn't care. I didn't have a boyfriend. In fact, I was single – a 'one-night stands' girl. I was known for doing those. I just wanted to feel loved even if it wasn't real. I gambled and took what was offered to me.

That night, my best friend and I were ready for the Kappa Ball. We arrived at the party looking stunningly gorgeous as always, and let's not forget classy. We were always on point and known as the "STUCK UP PRETTY GIRLS" around campus. Our names were in plenty females and males' mouths so showing up at the party looking fabulous made it even worse. They talked about us more, and the hate was real. We didn't let that stop us from shining, so the show went on.

I ran into one of my *friends with benefits*. We started talking and we danced, and we had drinks and more drinks. I drank so much until I didn't remember how we got to where we ended up. We were both out of it. All I remember was leaving the party, telling my best friend, *I'm leaving,* and *you know what I got up my sleeves.* We looked at each other and laughed. When I woke up the next morning, I was in a hotel room. We were both undressed so I didn't assume sexual encounters took place, I knew for sure it happened.

I was a loose woman. It was so dangerous to live that way. I was wild indeed, but God still had his angels camped around me. I encourage you not to be that way. It's not a good look for a woman to participate in such behavior. I didn't know any better. No one taught me. This behavior was something I experienced on my own. Now that I know better, I'm here to stop you. Save you from behaviors that may leave you with an STD or DEAD.

When I went back home that morning, my grandmother asked me a million questions. She was concerned. I knew she cared because if she didn't, she wouldn't have drilled me the way that she did. But I couldn't tell her what went on in the wee hours of the night I was gone. She would not have looked at me the same, so I lied to get her off my back. To tell you the truth, I wasn't a good liar. I came up with something so quick and fast, it didn't really make sense to me and I knew she didn't believe me. I could tell from her facial expression. She walked off.

I went into my cave (My Room) closed up in there preparing myself for the week of school. I had assignments stacked over my head. I knew it had to be done. Everything was due by that Monday morning and it wasn't going to get done by itself. Moves had to be made and normally I don't procrastinate. However, I'm always ahead.

I still didn't do right. I called my *other friend with benefits* over. We talked, we chilled, one thing led to another. I had performed my second one-night-stand in less than two days. And the fact that I knew he had a girlfriend didn't bother me one bit. My heart was so cold; all I was thinking about was getting what I wanted. It wasn't a need. I just wanted to add some more fire to the previous pleasure I had received hours ago. KARMA IS REAL. It didn't hit me right then and there but eventually karma came around for me to be served and it didn't feel good.

> *Never ever thinks It's OKAY to be involved with another woman's man. Once he is done with you, he will go back to her leaving you WET, EMPTY and LONELY.*

The pleasure of getting laid over and over gave me a high, to crave for every good feeling that I could feel and think of. I was becoming a "SEX ADDICT" and was very unaware of it. I was dying inside for a touch that I never felt before. For love I never received before, only to end up hurt and broken from doing all the wrong things to gain attention that were never right to begin with. I didn't know who I was becoming but I was slowly turning into a different person. Losing myself to be pleased. Falling into the lust of desires that had my soul swimming in sin. Causing me to just give up on God, leaving Him out of everything. Giving the devil permission of my soul, and he took me through it too. I was so lost I didn't think there was a way to escape from the devil's wills and ways. My life was finished.

If you noticed that you are thriving to feel that touch, that high, you may be becoming a Sex Addict - a slave - doing any and everything to feel that rush of pleasure. A drug will keep you coming back for more. You are self-destructing; not knowing your life is ending slowly.

Spring break came. I was elated. I needed a break from family, men, school, and just life period so my mom and I took a week of vacation to Atlanta, Georgia to visit my sister and her two children. It was time to reunite since we never had family reunions. It was a must that we love on one another and spend time together especially living so far apart.

My biggest fear was traveling. Oh, how I despised it. All of that sitting made me so uncomfortable. The whole time we were riding, I was complaining. It really got on my mom's nerves. As me and Mom talked, we caught up on the past, trying to figure out why things happen the way they did at the time I was birthed into this world. That talk was really emotional and tense until she fell asleep on me. I guess I was asking too many questions. Being there in each other's presence really brought us closer to one another.

I grew up without my mom so every time we were together, I took advantage of the time and cherished every moment. I didn't give up, but I kept fighting because of what I missed out on. The relationship with your mother is so important. If you don't have one yet, get to know each other and love on one another as if it's your last time.

We stopped in Jackson, Mississippi to switch buses. I woke my mom up to explain to her that we had to get off the bus and tell her that I didn't see my menstrual cycle for a few days. Although, I was cramping I didn't see any signs of blood. She insisted that it could be stress. I didn't know which was worse, me pondering about stress or me possibly being with child. My head was swimming. Then she said, "Wait. Be still. Let me check your pulse."

She put her finger under my neck. "Oh, you are fine," she said. "I only hear one heartbeat."

I said, "WHEEEEWWW. THANK YOU, JESUS!" At this point of my life, I was trying to complete my bachelor's degree. I didn't have time for babies. Besides, I couldn't even keep up with myself let alone a child.

The bus driver announced over the loud speaker, "Atlanta, Georgia." We finally arrived at our destination after sitting for 10 hours. That ride had me drained, but when I began to see how beautiful the city was, energy began to burst through me. Plus, I was excited that we made safe travels. God kept us out of harm's way while traveling down those dangerous highways.

We waited for my sister to pick us up from the bus station. While sitting there, I saw so many homeless individuals and families sleeping on the sidewalks. My heart sank. I felt so emotional. I'm going to school to be a social worker and all I could think about was getting back home to finish school. I needed to make a difference in the world. My voice had to be heard as an advocate for the ones who can't speak for themselves.

God wanted me to see those people in that situation. That scene opened my eyes up to life during a time when I was a "complainer". I had been complaining about everything. Nothing ever satisfied me. When I saw the homeless, it humbled me. I thanked God for everything I had.

> *Whatever situation you are in, be grateful because there is someone out there right now who would love to trade places with you. They have nothing yet we complain about the basics. Be mindful how life can change within a blink of an eye. But because God's grace is always sufficient, we can say we are blessed and highly favored.*

I decided to take a nap because I was exhausted. That ride was extremely long, and the minute I closed my eyes, I began to dream:

My Mom and I were walking towards the Fairground. One of the rides started to operate. It came scooping down low to the ground right where we were standing. The ride almost knocked us over. In a field somewhere, we began to walk towards some cars. We ended up on a Church ground. As we began to get in one of the cars, we saw two men shooting but they were mainly aiming for me. I kept trying to get in the car, but Mom got in and locked the doors. I started to run and finally found a hiding place. The men found me and shot me in the head. I still didn't die but I pretended that I was dead as the blood flowed from my head. They spotted me again and shot me in the leg. God insisted that I remain very still as they were so determined to kill me, they ran out of bullets. I was still alive walking as if nothing happened to me. God breathed new life into me.

My mom shook me! I jumped. I thought to myself, *man what was all that about?* This dream was furious. I couldn't function. My sister came in the room trying to plan a fun filled day, but I wasn't interested. My mind was so far off, I didn't know what to expect or what God was trying to tell me overall.

IT WAS A BLAST! Georgia was tons of fun, laughter, love, hugs, smiles, shopping etc. We had such a lovely time, but reality started to kick in. I had to get back to my life and school. There was no time to be wasted. I had to get on board because in two more months I would be walking across the stage. Everything was packed and ready to head back to Cleveland, Mississippi.

We made it back home. I didn't attend school that day. The bus ride was so tiring; I needed to get more rest. I called my cousin to take me to Burger King. I just had to have me a Whopper with cheese and a vanilla milk shake, ummmm ummm good. I bought my food, ate it, and I rested. I tossed and turned but eventually I ended up drifting off to sleep. I felt so sick. My stomach was doing all kinds of flips - a feeling I never felt before. I ignored it, until after I woke up. I felt a flutter, and all I kept thinking was *what they put in that food? My stomach was messed up.* My grandma insisted I had food poisoning. She told me to see a doctor. As much as I hated to look at them, I refused that offer and prayed to God about it. I just wanted that feeling to disappear.

A knock came on the door. To my surprise, it was my aunt asking me about the trip. In the middle of our conversation, she stopped and said, "You know you are glowing."

I said, "Who, not me?"

"You must be pregnant?"

I'm like, "Heck no.

"You sure look like it."

I told her what I had experienced after I finished eating my food.

She looked at me, "Food don't make you flutter. Let's go get a pregnancy test."

IT'S POSITIVE! I sat there in a daze; my mind haywire. I can't even describe the thoughts that ran through my brain. My heart sank.

Later that night, I called to tell my second *friend with benefits* that I was expecting. I assumed he was happy because he left his job to come comfort me. When he arrived, he hugged me. I freaked out and told him to get off me. I felt like a fool. I'm pregnant with another woman's man's child. I would have to quit school. My life on hold, dreams, visions, and goals - what must I do? Karma!

Decisions had to be made and quick! NOT to mention my priorities were not where they needed to be. But soon they would have to get in-check. My life was already deformed and the signs of being a single mom took place the same day I was left to raise a child alone.

Single Mom

As my journey began, I started to fall in very dark places. I knew I couldn't give up on life because I was carrying a life inside of me. "A Blessing in Disguise", that's what I called it. This "Blessing" had me pondering about how my life would change. Will it be for the better or the worse? I was thinking either way I was going to love this child with every ounce of love I had in me. I sat there with tears in my eyes. My mind was all over the place and my thoughts were draining me. The way my life was messed up I just couldn't fathom bringing a baby in the world.

My phone went off as my favorite ringtone played. A text message came through. Before I could even read all of it, my heart was already breaking. I continued to scroll. The friend with benefits who's now my child's father begins to say he didn't want any dealings with me anymore and that I should have an abortion. He was even willing to pay for it. He knew how bad I wanted a family, but the way things were going, that was most certainly out of the question. He was very disturbed about this child.

My pain sank so deep, I fell into depression. I thought I was slowly losing my mind, drifting into a daze. The fact that he decided to be a "Boyfriend" to someone else and not a "Father" to the child I carried baffled me – somewhat. Now I had to do this with no help. I had no hope.

> *Often times we want what we can't have and if we play around with it too long, we will start to see it was never in God's plan to begin with. For most of us, as long as we try to plan our lives without God, the worse it will get and never work out; certain to fail every time.*

My stomach was growing, my face was spreading, and my body was going through changes. I loved being pregnant simply because I was never sick, I could eat any and everything I craved, and it never upset my stomach. That was the best part of my pregnancy. Of course, I'm a food lover and I loved to eat, and still do. It was awesome. Well until my sleeping pattern started to go another route. I loss much sleep due to stress and worrying trying to figure out life nearly drove me into a coma, especially thinking how I will be able to provide for a child when I can barely provide for myself. Times were really hard for me, each day I went through the motion with no support, no love, and no encouragement. I picked up my bible every now and then. I even felt as if God wasn't there but that wasn't the case. I didn't let Him in, and because of that, I went through. Hell! I suffered, I cried, I felt alone, I was depressed I was so low. I had low self-esteem, even as blessed as I was with looks. But when someone put in your head how worthless and unimportant you are, those thoughts ride and never stop moving.

After Spring break, for that last two weeks I still attended College at Delta State University, but no one noticed my growing stomach, and to be honest I didn't want them to. I was really ashamed. I informed my instructors that I had to withdraw for family issues and being with child caused a lot of chaos and much confusion. They all tried to convince me to stay. I knew I wouldn't have the help and support I needed so I had no other choice but to stop. I didn't give up. I searched and searched the web to find an accredited online school. That way when I transferred it wouldn't be a problem. I was blessed to find one, Brescia University. I called made arrangements, did all the paper worked they needed and three weeks later, I received a letter in the mail I was accepted into the school. Not only that, I was accepted into the Social Work Program.

Your dreams may look like it will end at that moment, but that end can be a new way to a better opportunity. When one door closes, it's a fact that God will make a way to open another door for you to get where you need to be. Keep pressing, you are almost there.

But I had another problem. I know me and Asher had broken up and we hadn't talked to each other for like eight or nine months, so I was very afraid to tell him I was pregnant with another man's baby. I knew how he felt about me. On top of that, I never told him about the miscarriage. This secret was eating me alive. I delivered the message to "our brother", Cody. I could talk to him about anything. He was my personal Dr. Phil. I always had an ear full to tell him. It was something new every day. As I was coming through the Student Union, he saw me and called my name. No way could I do anything but cry. Venting to him, letting him know I didn't know how to tell Asher this heartbreaking news. He calmed me down rubbing my stomach making me laugh and he told me he would sit Asher down and tell him. I was so scared I didn't want to see him around campus. Every time I saw him, I dodged him and went the opposite way. It was just that bad.

I knew Cody had my back, he's my Ace. I loved him like a real brother, and he loved me too. We had a bond unbreakable. I was on my way home and before I could get in the door good, I received a text message from Asher. He had been angry all day and he even shed tears. After Cody had delivered the message to Asher, he called. I knew I had hurt him. I answered the phone in tears. All I could hear him say, "I'm still in love with you and even though that baby isn't mine, we are going to be together."

I kept telling him no I did enough damage. He said, "God will see us through." We expressed how much we loved one another and hung up the phone. I needed to stay focused, to clear my mind for assignments that were due shortly. I never experienced online school before my enrollment, but it was wonderful. People made it sound so harsh and boring. I loved it. Everything was right there in place. I just had to be persistent, dedicated, devoted, and determined, which I didn't have a problem with. School was my desire, and whatever I had to do for my child I was willing and able to put my heart, mind, body, and soul into it so I could be the best I can.

My first assignment was due by midnight. I finished it and went to bed. I had a doctor's appointment the next day. I was nervous about going to the doctor; nevertheless, I was happy I'd find out how my child was doing. I was always alone on my visits, but I had company this time - the father came along. If I couldn't count on him to be with me any other doctor visits, I sure could this time. It was time to find out if it's a boy or a girl, so yeah of course. Why would he miss this moment? Time was really passing by and I was four months pregnant on June 28, 2012. I will never forget. My heart burst with joy when I found out we were having a girl. Instantly falling in love, another image of me was forming life inside of my womb; preparing to come into the world.

No one understood the pain as I faced so many issues alone. This child could have brought the best or the worse out of me, but through it all, I had to stay strong, fight, and for sure keep God first. I knew He would get me where I needed to be in life if I yielded to Him submissively. I had to take it one thought at a time; just to live in comfort and be content. It was a big challenge, but I survived and found joy in the midst of my pain. It didn't feel good; it was a press as well as a push to know that I was in this by myself. Not knowing how it would turn out. I didn't know which way to go but I had to make a choice to try to fix it on my own or I had to turn to God, the one I turned my back on. If I didn't need Him then, I surely needed Him this time around. This battle was too much for me to handle. I asked God to forgive me, coming with a heart of repentance, giving Him every trouble I was dealing with. I was willing to have a free mind from all that was going on.

No matter how much you sin, God is always there to pick you up when you fall. He gives you the strength and peace you need. When you are weak, He will love you, healing you when you alone. Keep Him first and invite Him in everything. Never leave Him out and trust Him with any situation at hand.

Although Asher vowed to get back with me, karma showed up in my life, too. He was very bitter towards me, answering the phone when he wanted to, and calling when he got ready. I figured someone else had his attention. Things were just not the same. I can say he did give me moral support as I carried this baby. He couldn't be there physically, but he cared for and loved this baby as much as I did. My life was flipping upside down and I was paining for doing wrong and making wrong decisions.

School began to wear me down mentally. My pregnancy took a real big toll on me. I would be up all night at my computer desk doing work. I loved to stay ahead. I didn't care how tired I was, I wouldn't be satisfied until all of my schoolwork was completely finished. The work seemed never-ending. Tests, pop quizzes, papers, and must I add more papers, and questions but I made it through. I worked hard, I applied myself, and I did what was required of me. I had goals set so getting everything accomplished on time made me reach for the stars, grabbing whichever ones had the most opportunities that would line up with my dreams. I was willing to pull down whatever God had for me.

Don't stop, keep going. You must fight to be successful. You are almost there. Enjoy where

*you are to get where you are going. The
milestone is worth every tear you shared, every
late night you didn't get sleep. Continue to work
hard.*

At the time, I was a worrier. I worried about everything,
but when you care to a certain level, you can expect to think
more than you should. Mainly being concerned with trying
to prepare for the *what ifs*, the *disappointments*, the *let
downs*, and the *no's*. Each month as the baby grew, I could
see my feet less and less. Of course, my problems were
expanding too. The closer I came to the end of my
pregnancy, the more fear I had. Fear of my future. Fear of
my suffering. Fear of my dedication to my child. Fear of
being a failure. Fear of not being prepared as a single mom.
The list went on and on. It had to be done. I vowed to take
the heartaches, the loneliness, the mental abuse, and verbal
abuse, and although all these things made me feel worthless
and unimportant, I still held on to it to build strength in my
character. I needed to do this. It helped me face my
insecurities, my flaws, rejection of wanting to be loved but
being misused. I learned how to be alone without family and
the craving of wanting to be with a man.

*If you don't deal with your flaws and how
someone treats you, those issues will deal with
you, causing you more pain than you can handle.
It will never go away. Only God Himself can heal
you from the scattered broken pieces that
damaged you.*

My due date was November 11, 2012. This is the day we (my family and me) were expecting our baby girl to make her grand entrance in the world. But things changed suddenly. We were sitting around talking and laughing. I laughed so hard, I started to hurt. I was on my way to lie down when I thought about my school project and paper that was almost due. I needed God on both ends for the pain, the project, and the paper. My work was due in a week. Mind you, I'm just on page two. I needed my rest but I sacrificed my sleep. I went in my zone to block all the noises out and the rest of the world by listening to music. Music always soothes me, taking me to another level.

I began to type when thoughts started to flow. Everything was pulling together. I finished my project and my paper. I stayed up until 3:00 a.m. practically all night. I was determined. I thank God for giving me the strength. I fell asleep and woke up about five that morning heading to the refrigerator looking for food. After searching for something to eat, I decided to take a shower. I prayed while in the shower to ease my mind. I laid back down again, this time reading my Bible. I remember reading The Book of Revelations. As I went deeper into my reading, I began to fear, and I felt my heart racing.

I asked myself is this really how the world is going to be, and then he spoke to me. Normally when God speaks, I'm never heeding but I took heed this time. He said, *Warning Before Destruction. Watch your surroundings and the people you are hanging with. It's time to get right. I'm on my way back.*

I was furious because I wasn't in the Lord like I needed to be, so I didn't understand. I began to prepare for how the rest of my day would be. In fact, I had my whole day planned out. In the midst of all that, God spoke to me again. He said, *You are about to encounter a new beginning.*

I got excited. I just knew all that dedication, hard work, and sleepless nights were about to pay off. But that wasn't it. I fell asleep once again, this time waking up at 11:27 a.m. I rushed out of bed. "Oh my goodness," I screamed, telling my grandma I'm peeing everywhere. She jumped up explaining to me my water had broken. The baby was on the way. I guess the laughter and the Wendy's Chili earlier the night before had done it for me. I was in labor. *Little old me was getting ready to have a baby.*

I was calm but my grandma on the other hand not so much. She was acting like she was having the baby. She tried to call everyone to take me to the hospital, but all the phones were powered off. We had one last option, our neighbor. She insisted that I ride with him. I said, "Oh no that truck is too raggedy. What if it cuts off in the middle of the highway?"

She said, "Well you will have the baby right there."

My aunt arrived in town, pulling up just in time. I didn't let her get in the driveway good. I walked extremely fast getting in her vehicle. The pains started to get unbearable. I couldn't stand it. We made it to the hospital in less than ten minutes. I was so nervous. This was something I was prepared for. I was about to take care of another life besides my own.

The nurses rolled me up to my designated area. It was hard contacting the father of my child, so my family assisted me until he arrived. I have never been a fan of pain and those contractions were kicking my butt! I was in labor for eight plus hours until I decided on the Epidural.

After the procedure was done, the pain relieved. I was smiling and not feeling a thing. I was sitting thinking of my sister because she wasn't there to experience that moment with me, and I wasn't having my baby until I spoke with her over the phone. She was on the road and I was in labor. We were both going in different directions. She finally called me. Someone had given her the memo that her niece was on the way. As soon as I hung up the phone, the doctor came in to check me. He told me, "It's time!"

They rolled me down the hall into the delivery room. The nurses asked me to spread my legs as far as they could go. After more delivery instructions, I pushed, pushed, and pushed. Baby girl was positioned to come out, but we had one problem. She wasn't on one accord with me. She was stuck in my right side debating whether she wanted to come out. They ask me to push again. I obeyed. I pushed, taking deep breaths; nothing still. The doctor came in saying I had to get a Cesarean (C-Section). I cried, I did not want to get cut on but I couldn't risk my child's life or my own life so that calmed me. The staff prepared me for surgery. They told me to relax, and they laughed and joked with me until I drifted off to sleep. The minute I closed my eyes I saw God. He said, *Don't be afraid.*

Just knowing I was lying there cut wide open was terrifying but Glory be to God, we both survived. I opened my eyes and my new beginning was in my face crying. That was October 27, 2012 at 5:46 p.m. I had a girl who was HEAVEN SENT. My aunt named her Zion Za'nae!

Becoming a Mother was nothing I could prepare for, although I was honored to be Zion Mother. Being a single mother was the hardest trail I endured. There were times that I would go into a deep depression, not knowing how I would get through it alone. I could never have imagined facing such difficult moments. I didn't even expect to have her out of wedlock. I always desired to be married but unfortunately, it didn't happen that way. My whole life changed as I transitioned from self-centeredness, "It's all about me" to selflessness, "It's no longer about me." My child had to come first. Growing out of those ways were very painful, but I made the sacrifice as I hurt and cried progressing to be the best mother I could be for my child. After all, she didn't ask to be here so I had to step it up with responsibility, priorities, and perseverance. I did whatever I needed to do to make sure she wasn't without because she depended on me to be there every step of the way.

> *No child is a mistake or an accident, but motivation. In spite of how they got here, children are still a blessing. You can make it. Embrace each day.*

Zion's father and I were in a very bad space. Not talking, both of us stubborn as a mule, which made it so much harder to get alone. We were always at each other's throat. We just couldn't pull it together for Zion so that caused me to depend more on God, depend on government assistance, and be independent as much as possible. Not to mention, I wasn't receiving child support at that time. The help I did get was a necessary blessing. I wasn't working nor was I in school. It seemed like everything besides motherhood was on hold. I was still trying to find my way. I thought to myself. *I'm a Mom now. Time to get in preparation.* But in reality, there was nothing to prepare for. I just had to do it, learn, understand, and move ahead. As the days went by, I did what needed to be done just to be able to protect and provide. My mind was set, and I was ready.

Zion was growing rapidly. I never in my life have seen such a beautiful little girl. She made my heart smile every time I stared obsessively. And I had to look at her to keep from crying. I felt that my situation wasn't fair. How I was treated was damaging to me, causing me so much stress. I wanted better. I wasn't supported. I wasn't getting help. It was much chaos in the midst of my home and I really felt like everyone was against me.

When Zion was seven months old, I packed our stuff up and left Cleveland, MS (along with my mom) headed to Atlanta, GA. We waited for the bus to pull off, and waving goodbye to family and friends, tears began to fall. The whole bus ride, I cried and prayed asking God, *"Lord I'm ready for a new start. I'm ready for change. I stepped out on faith with no money just my child, my mom, and myself. I'm a single mom, a sinner who needs your assistance as we travel to this big city to make a living. I love you God. Thank you for listening to a sinner's prayer. Amen"*

I was always known to branch out so I wasn't nervous or afraid. That's how courageous and strong I am. In fact, I was happy to be in a new area just to see a new environment, with a new scenery, new people, places, and opportunities. I was overwhelmed with joy, ready for newness and because I trusted God, I knew He was going to make a way. I didn't know how, when, or where but with Him, all things were possible if I would just believe. We lived in this new area with my sister. She allowed us to stay with her until better came our way.

When we arrived, things weren't what they appeared to be. What I thought was a new beginning ended very fast. My situation became worse and I couldn't understand why things were happening like they were. I was confused because I had left a home I knew and walked right into an already bad situation. I was just stuck. I wasn't in the Lord like I should have been, but I was in the process of drawing closer to Him. I was lost and when He spoke, there was no way I could hear Him. I was sinning, leaning on thin prayers that made me miss out on the move of God and the instructions he had set up for me.

> *Never run from your problems. Either you add more or God will allow you to go through something way worse. Running into something you can't handle; the problem will be so bad you can only go to God for peace and understanding. The normal calamity you create is because of disobedience, so deal with it and come out victoriously.*

Provisions were slowly being made. I was living in a city that I always wanted to live in, but more importantly, go to school in. This was my chance to go after everything my heart desired. I loved that it didn't take long to get use to Georgia. I adapted to the fast life quicker than I thought. There was so much to do, so many opportunities; I didn't know where to start. As I sat on the floor doing what I love to do – write – and planning my next move, I looked up and someone was putting a key in the door. Now I'm pondering because this is my sister's apartment, which is what she told me before we arrived. So why was someone sticking a key in the door, entering as if they lived there?

A woman walked in the door with her nose in the air. She didn't speak, just looked at me, and went to a bedroom. I went to my sister and interrupted her phone conversation. "Who is the lady that just walked in the house?"

She said, "My roommate."

I'm like, "Wait a minute, so this isn't your own apartment?"

She replied, "No."

Instantly, I got an attitude. We argued because she beat around the bush on the phone because she knew if I had known then what I found out later, I wouldn't have stepped foot in Georgia. That night was full of chaos. After all that, I had to get me a drink. I didn't care what it was. My mind was flowing, and I needed something to calm me down from those insane thoughts. I wanted to kill everybody in the house including myself, but thankfully those thoughts went away, and I drifted off to sleep.

I woke up the next morning thinking to myself, *What have I done? I came here to make a better life and things were out of order.* I started to question did I do the right thing; was it the right time? The right move? To just leave because nothing had happened for me just yet? All that pondering caused me to have a massive headache. Head hurting as if it didn't want to stop. To clear my mind, I dressed my daughter and we started our day. The way I felt, I needed some sort of release to keep me focused. We walked over to the lake with my niece and nephew. I always enjoyed watching the water and hearing it flow smoothly. As the wind blew, more intense, whispering tears began to fall down my face uncontrollably. I was lost; my mind was out of it trying to be found. As the kids ran back up where I stood, I hurried to wipe the tears away.

Mom called us in to eat. While we waited for our meal, I grew excited about how much I loved food. Food made me happy. However, as the plates were being fixed, my sister and her roommate argued over the AC unit. The roommate didn't want any air on, and she did it to be spiteful because not only was it hot outside it was babies in the house including my seven-month-old daughter. The evil person that she was, she cut the wires to the unit so no one could use it, and all hell broke loose. My sister was about to beat her into a coma. It was so hot outside and we were drained and dehydrated. My daughter started to turn red in the face. I had to give her lots of water and ice to keep her body cool. As I walked the kids downstairs, following the direction of the officer, this lady told us we can sit in her car. I was skeptical at first, but my baby needed air, so I took the offer.

We talked about the situation that took place for about an hour or two and in the midst, I asked her name.

"Seven."

As the officer resolved the matter, Seven asked if we wanted to stay with her until all the issues were taken care of. I agreed. To take the focus off the problem, I began to stare in the sky obsessively day dreaming - mind in space. The car pulled off. I jumped and started to notice how beautiful Georgia really was. I looked around and I could see that living there would be great. I just wanted a better life for my daughter and me.

I was truly at ease, knowing that my child and I had been taken away from so much drama. Many burdens were lifted. She showed me to the room that we would sleep in and the rest of the house. As I got acquainted with this house, I noticed it was so warm, and even though I'd only been there for a few hours, I felt welcomed and loved. I knew it was nobody but God simply because I stepped out on faith with no money; just my child and my belongings. In the midst of all that chaos, God made a way for me to still live there and be at peace with the situation.

> Never be scared to branch out. God knows what you going to do before you do it, and when you do step out on faith, He will be sure to take care of you.

I get attached to people extremely fast and I was there for maybe two days at the most. I was relaxed, comfortable, and really feeling the vibe and to be honest I did not want to go back to where I was living – with my sister. I despised being there so being the blunt, straightforward person I am, with no hesitation; I asked Seven if my daughter and I could make this our new home. At least until God saw fit for us to have our own. She didn't mind; she even said yes but had to ask her husband's permission. As we stalled time sitting around getting to know one another on a personal level, laughing joking, eating having a good time, her husband, the detective, walked in the door. It was his first time seeing us due to his hacked work schedule. He spoke going upstairs for a few minutes. He came back down and we talked. He drilled me but in a good way. He did more of the talking and I had no problem with it. Because of the person I am, it just put more confidence in me to finish what I started.

> *When someone sees that you have good intentions about life, they will inspire you and encourage you to do more, so you can be great in every aspect of your days of living.*

I needed to be in that house. I know God placed them in my life for a reason. I knew they would help me get where God was intending me to be. He insisted that I could move in. I was elated with joy. This was a new beginning to a fresh start to get into preparation to make provision to do something different. We instantly hopped in the car to go back to the place I was living to pack all my things. I left and didn't turn back. Even though I was a sinner, I saw God move His unchanging hands, Him facing and guiding me to a new route that could possibly lead me to new opportunities. Life was starting to fall in place. Eventually, I would have gotten where I needed to be if I kept the faith, stood firm and kept God first always. Everything was starting to look up for me, I think. Transitions seemed like they were taking place.

As I worked hard to find a job and finish my B.S. degree in social work, moves were being made as if I was getting somewhere but I didn't see any results still. I started to wonder and question God. I didn't understand why I felt stagnant, why things were not looking up for me. I was doing right, making the necessary steps to get ahead to be successful.

The worse feeling any human being can feel is not hearing from God when you poured your heart out to get answers. It's like He turned His back on you because you're yet still a sinner, still disobeying. *What must I do?* The days went by and I was still strategizing, planning to live better and be a better woman. I began to do my research on colleges. I ran across a school located in Griffin, Georgia, University of Georgia - UGA, that was accredited, ranked in the top 5 schools in Georgia and just what I needed, they also had a Social Work Program. I was very excited and called the school to make a tour. I was thrilled. *This could be my big break; a chance I get the degree I've been longing for; possibly get my career started; heading for the future doing what I love.*

After I scheduled the tour, I didn't stop there. I was still looking for colleges, filling out as many applications as I could. Just in case Plan A didn't work out, I had Plan B to fall back on. School was what my heart mostly desired and I wasn't stopping until I reached my level of excellence.

Being in Georgia was a blessing and a curse. God was there, but I wasn't doing well. I felt as If I failed God, and by doing that really woke me up. Life isn't a fairytale, it's real. I was living in reality and I was so used to things being done for me that facing life on my own was harder than I thought. But I always applauded myself for taking the risk and being courageous enough to even come to a big city, especially coming from a small town. Although, I learned lessons and I went through tough times, God was still there with me holding my hand, guiding me through every step. I still enjoyed Atlanta, Georgia, such a beautiful city. I loved every bit of it.

Somehow, all my enjoyment went out the window July 12, 2013. I was excited and sad, mixed emotions everywhere. I had just finished my tour with UGA. They showed me so much love I was filled with joy knowing that I only needed one class to get accepted into the school and the Social Work Program. They even offered me schools to apply for to get that one class done so I could start in the fall. However, sadly I couldn't. After a long day of touring my future school, I took a nap. The minute I closed my eyes, I dreamed:

My daughter and I were standing in the middle of nowhere when a fire blazed up. It was coming towards us. I'm certain the world was about to end the way the fire was looking. I covered my daughter. I didn't care about getting burned up. I just wanted her safe. The fire got closer and closer, and I heard people screaming and crying out for help. As the fire began to do a big explosion, God took my soul clean out my body leaving me lifeless while my daughter stood there lost.

My phone vibrated and I jumped. I miss that call, waking up to 13 other missed calls and many text messages. I was so disturbed with my dream I still didn't answer the phone because now I'm thinking God is about to take me off the face of this earth. I'm still sinning. I'm not living right. It's time to give my life to God is what I was thinking. I was troubled and fearful. The phone ring again. This time I picked up. As my aunt took a deep breath, I could feel that it was some bad news because of my dream. She said, "Skyye, she's gone."

"Who's gone?"

"Mom," was her response.

I stood there in total shock. My whole body went numb. I began to pain instantly. I just hung up the phone, not to mention I'm going through a break-up of three plus years trying to heal from that now this. Lord, what am I going to do? I can barely stand a needle sticking me. I hate pain let alone dealing with another Scar, another wound, of my heart being broken twice. Lord, where are you? I need you.

I was sitting. I didn't shed one tear. I was in denial. I couldn't take in that she was no longer living. The last time we talked, it wasn't pretty. I never got a chance to tell her I loved her. The conversation ended with her hanging up in my face. The pain was too much to bear. I wanted to die. I didn't sleep for a week. I was anxious, nervous, and confused because I had to return home to a funeral to say my final goodbye.

I looked for bus tickets in advanced so our tickets could already be purchased when time to attend the funeral. In my heart, I couldn't believe that my grandmother had passed. It didn't sit well with me at all. I was so thrown off, I forgot about my dreams, visions, and goals. I checked out of life for a long period of time. I really had to find myself; do some soul searching because if I didn't, they were going to be planning a funeral for me soon. The suicidal thoughts continuously raged my mind. It was too much on my plate, dealing with the death of a loved one and suffering pain from a long-term relationship had me mentally insane, stressed, bothered, hurt. I was so vulnerable if someone wanted to take advantage of me, they would have done it and ran with it. Life was very stormy, and the storms came without warnings, which cause every piece of me to be broken.

As the days went by, I tried to cope with knowing I'm going back to an empty house, no food cooking on the stove, no blues playing on the radio, no family gatherings, no chaos, no drama. Just to know that she wasn't going to be there was going to be a hard pill to swallow. I dreaded packing. I was skeptical as to staying in Georgia or moving back home. I was torn between the two. I knew I didn't have the help or the support there, so I instantly changed my mind. I loved where I was living. That house became our home. I finally started packing making sure I had everything I needed to take to Mississippi. Seven asked me if was I ready to go. I breathed calmly and said yes, I'm ready.

Heading to the bus station, mind overloaded with concerns for my life, my daughter, my family. So much was going on, I couldn't think straight. I wanted to drift off into a deep sleep and never return, but I knew my daughter needed me, so I had to shake that feeling off. It wasn't the right time to be in that state of mind. I had to be strong for my daughter. I just wanted to get this over with so I could rest.

Patterns

We arrived at the bus station, making our way back to Mississippi. My family was waiting on our arrival. I knew they missed us. We had been gone for nearly three months and to tell the truth, I missed my family as much as they missed us. The bus pulled off and Seven said with a big smile that made me feel a little better, "Call me when you guys make it there."

Riding down the highway, night fell quickly, and I couldn't see anything. All I could do was look up to the sky and stare at the small stars. They were so bright; tears began to roll down my face. My phone vibrated interrupting my peace. It was Marlow calling to check on me, but I really didn't think that was the real reason for the call. I knew what he wanted because I wanted the same thing. I was frustrated, lost, and confused. *A release would do me some good right now.* He'd never seemed this concerned about me before. Well maybe he's pretending. I don't know, but whatever games he was trying to play I was certain this game was about to be very interesting. We ended the conversation with me letting him know when I would arrive so he could pick me up. He had already purchased the hotel room.

I never understood why I would give in to him knowing all he wanted from me was sex. I guess because I needed to feel alive and wanted. He gave me the attention, but it was always in the wrong areas, and what I was going through, attention was necessary. It didn't matter that I was a side chick, a jump-off, a rebound; I just wanted to feel loved and I was - in the worst ways. I gambled a lot with my life. I took chances that I knew would have my heart buried in the ground.

My baby girl had fallen asleep on me. The bus ride soon was lonely, and my bored mind over-filled with thoughts that I couldn't control. The phone was extremely dry, so I powered it off and laid there thinking about why my life had turned out this way. I even questioned God if this was His will. My life seemed to have hit rock bottom, and everything was going in a slow steady pace. I couldn't escape from the despair. I constantly walked around with this hurt that I couldn't understand or identify. During these stages of hurt or loneliness, I would talk and cry my heart out to God. I didn't realize that every time I did, it was an inner healing therapy for me, and in most situations, it helped.

It was almost daylight and I noticed the sign, WELCOME TO MISSISSIPPI! I knew we were close to home. We arrived to a hot summer only to find that I really didn't have a home anymore. I lived in that house for more than twenty-two years. Not once did I think I would be making my last visit to see my grandmother. Life felt so hopeless. I had had suicidal thoughts about killing myself several times. I always thanked God for not allowing me to attempt that act. But I did start to hate myself; partly taking the blame why she was gone. Guilty feelings swelled up in me because I left home at a time when she was healing from grieving the loss of her loved one.

The bus ride ended as we pulled up to our designated area. As I called for our ride home, my depression kicked in very fast. I looked down at my phone. Three missed calls popped up. Marlow had called to see if I had made it in. I didn't call back, instead I texted him my whereabouts. He could visit me later.

Riding down the street towards home just didn't feel the same anymore. The closer we came to the house the sicker I became. I got out of the vehicle and stood up and I threw up everywhere. It really hit hard that my grandmother was gone. It took me about an hour to go in the house as my family comforted and coached me. Finally, I built up my nerves to walk inside. It was very foggy and a midst of cool breeze touched my body. I never in my life experienced such a feeling. I sat down and as Zion held on to me tight, she cried. She cried and cried, she grieved, and she knew something was wrong. When I took her back outside, she stopped crying instantly. As I comforted her with my love, hugs, and kisses, she smiled. I knew from her smile that she would be okay.

We went back in the house to eat and my phone rang again. *I'm so tired of this phone ringing I'm about to throw it out,* I thought before answering. It was Zion's dad. He asked if he could see her later that day. I said sure. I knew she missed him, but besides that, I was trying to get laid. I rushed him off the phone and I called Marlow to get me around eleven that night. He agreed. What I wanted was not what I needed. Habits soon became patterns that left me craving for more and more. Things were surely getting out of control.

Night fell. Everyone had left my grandmother's house and gone their separate ways. Marlow called me to see if I was ready. I needed a minute to get my daughter situated. I finally got her to sleep and asked my cousin to watch her for me; I expected for no more than two hours. I sent Marlow a text to be on his way to get me. While sitting waiting on him to show up, thoughts flowed through my head, *It's time to get right with God.* I said to that silent voice, "Not today."

I was just living in the moment, praying that God would forgive me for doing things that were not of Him. I knew what I was doing was wrong but every time my mind would go into a deep thought about having sex, my body would react to the signs of my lustful desires. I couldn't resist the feeling of wanting to be pleased. Time after time, I'd asked myself why I constantly put up with being this way. It seemed as if I wasn't tired of the pain because I found myself becoming addicted to it.

To my surprise, Marlow had me something to drink. I wasn't a heavy drinker, but I was down with drinking all my pain away and regretting it the next day. Life was starting to drain me. All I wanted was to wake up from this nightmare; to fill voids, and to deny the hurt. I was scarred and I had wounds yet healed but I still insisted that all this would fade away if I kept the pleasure going; the temporary happiness. The insincere smile that showed no signs of the brokenness took over. I was bleeding eternally, praying, and hoping to be freed from the pain of walking in darkness. I suffered depression, bitterness, fear, and confusion. Obviously, the demons in me were taking over. The strongholds became stronger. I didn't like the way I was living. I wanted to see the light and was so unsure how to do so. But I continued to do what I wanted with no remorse, no conscious, no guilt, and no shame; exactly what the devil wanted. I yielded to him whole-heartily, while trying to get close to God at the same time.

At the hotel, we rested and talked for a minute. He began kissing me on my neck, caressing my body, grabbing my inner thighs, doing whatever he wanted to do with me and to me. I didn't care. I wanted to feel that high of pleasure I'd been longing for. Time was of the essence. We didn't waste any time giving ourselves to one another. The more we had sex, the higher my sex drive thrilled through my body; craving for more. I knew then, it wasn't a habit, it was a pattern. But the way I was headed, sooner or later, I'd be a sex addict.

After having sex three times in less than an hour, my body was still sending signals that it wasn't enough. I sat there saying to myself, "I AM A SEX ADDICT". After all that took place, you would think I was burned out. I knew I had to get back home, and he had to do the same. As he dropped me off at my house, we said our goodbyes and my mind was clear. The frustration had gone away, and I felt alive. I enjoyed that high because I know in a matter of seconds that feeling would fade completely away and I'd be feeling right back empty.

My mind wondered in worry. The next day was the wake for my grandmother. I couldn't sleep. I stayed up half of the night listening to music and watching my daughter sleep peacefully. The morning came and I was as anxious as ever.

I was ready to get the day over with; the whole funeral process rather. As time went by, I started to write. Besides sex, writing was another form of releasing my pain. Anything I held inside, I would let my pen do the talking for me as my words poured from my heart.

I wrote maybe five poems to expand the time of the wake. Everyone was leaving, I was the last person to the car. I asked God to forgive me for the sins I committed the night before. I prayed to God to keep me, and give me the strength I needed to face this tough situation called death. We headed to the funeral home and I felt myself shaking. I was nervous. Sweat was popping off me like I stole something. I couldn't get my body to leave that car. They had to drag me into the funeral home. When I thought I was ready mentally, I wasn't.

I thought I was ready, trying to prep myself saying, "Okay Skyye, you can do this." However, I would tiptoe to the door and draw back saying, "I'm not ready," breathing heavily. I sat down by my cousin as her tears flowed, rocking back and forth. I tried it again. I went to the door, saw her beautiful flowers, and just fell to my knees. When I saw her body, I cried extremely hard. I got close to the casket, just staring in disbelief. But she was laying there so beautiful, resting in peace while I was in the process of finding peace. I rubbed her cold hard face as I remembered her smile to keep sane. I grabbed my daughter so she could see my grandmother for the last time. She said goodbye using her hand gestures. I burst out crying again because it touched my heart. I can't deny how stressful that day was for me. I didn't want to believe what I'd just seen. Life was so pointless to me at that moment. I wanted to die. I just couldn't see myself living. How would I be strong, how would I let go, how would I heal, how would I stop blaming myself for her death? So may questions with very few answers. I needed God because I was drowning in my sins. I was dying slowly and trying to keep my composure of taking on the responsibility of the death nearly killed me. I was lost and couldn't seem to find my way through life.

Afterwards, we all met back up at my grandmother's house to eat, sit, and talk. As everyone sit in the living room discussing memories of my grandmother, I closed myself in my soon-to-be old room. I spent last minutes and hours in it reminiscing on all the things that took place because it was most certain my last day being there. I prepared clothes for Zion and me for the funeral. Tears formed in my eyes. I never expected to say my goodbyes that way. It just wasn't right. I couldn't stomach the feeling. I got sick all of a sudden, so I laid down. I drifted off to sleep in a dark place of depression that kept me insanely disrupted. Thoughts all over the place, I needed things to go back to normal.

Now I'm waiting on her to open the door to play with Zion and to fuss at me because of me *sleeping my life away*. I sat there all night right at the door. She still didn't come I'm asking when will she crack this door… but a scream alarmed in me so loud. I pulled my hair because what I wanted to happen was no longer going to happen. I knew I needed to shake this feeling. I could have gone into an anxiety attack at any time. I cried again as reality really sat in on me. I tried my best to deal with this, Lord. I needed His help. I began to sweat. I was furious and scared barely able to breathe. A tingling feeling went through my arms. I was sure I was about to fall out. I started to pray, and God touched me and gave me the strength to feel better.

I had bags under my eyes from staying up all night. I was drained in every area, mentally, physically and emotionally. I couldn't get my daughter dressed for the funeral let alone myself, so my sister dressed Zion as I pulled myself together. I called Zion's daddy to see if he was on his way and because he knew how much of emotional creature I was, he was by my side supporting me in this most difficult time in life. He showed up and I hurried and got in the car so we wouldn't miss the direction of the traffic. We lined up for the funeral to get to the Church. At this point, I'm still not right in the mind. I'm in denial and I'm numb as I sat in the car shaking my leg. My stomach started to hurt. We had to line up to go into the Church. The line was moving faster than I thought and I was almost in the door. The tears formed and suddenly began to fall. I'm walking and walking covering my eyes because now I'm at the casket. I burst out with a loud scream. They say the loudest ones are those who are guilty of something or have done no good by that person. In my case, I was "The Guilty One". All I could replay in the back of my head is the argument that took place two days before her death. She cursed me out and hung up the phone in my face. I cried even louder breaking down to my knees. This can't be real. *I never got a chance to tell you I love* you is what I'm saying to the lifeless body that lay there not responding back.

That hurt me to the core. I was saddened, as the ceremony went on. I had been asked to read a poem and I just couldn't stand there. I was surely going to fall out so one of my Church members read the poem for me. My life was destined to change. I couldn't run from it, couldn't go around it, under it or through it. I had to face it if I wanted to heal.

Because I knew from that moment that it was purpose in the pain. I just had to dig through those so stressful times.

The funeral was finally over. We left the Church going next door to accompany family and friends in the fellowship hall to eat. I didn't have an appetite. I wasn't even in a position to be around people. I'm an introvert; a sure loner. I just wanted to be shut up in a dark room away from family and this cruel world. I just wanted to be left alone, but Zion's dad asked me to stay with him until we went back to Atlanta Georgia. I said yes because I needed a clear mind. It was so much hatred and strife between us; we needed to be on one accord or at least cordial for our daughter. So we talked, at least tried to get an understanding of the mess we created.

In the car, things went awry. We were always at each other's throats so I'm like *just forget it.* Whatever, this had to be put in God's hands. I didn't have the energy to live let along fighting and trying to be the bigger person; trying to make peace. *Something had to give.* We made it to his house and he asked me if I was hungry. I still didn't have an appetite, but he cooked food for Zion and me. I fed Zion, bathed her, and got her ready for bed and he insisted that I lay in his arms to feel comfortable. I hesitated at first. He kissed me all over then one thing led to another and before I knew it, we were having sex; something that I tried so hard to avoid. How things went before and after getting pregnant, I should have had enough of the hurt and pain, so now I'm about to go back to Georgia thinking about someone I can no longer be with. It was bad enough, we weren't together as a family, and having sex with him was so unhealthy making me cling to him more. I'm like *why do I keep doing this to myself.* It was clear that I was not only an addict to sex, now I have just discovered I was an addict to pain too.

We stayed up talking until we both fell asleep. The next time I open my eyes, it was morning. I probably had about two hours of sleep. I can say when I woke up, I felt like a brand-new person. Maybe I did need the sex, but I knew if I kept holding on to those feelings and that temporary high of pleasure would have me crazy in the head and craving for more sex. The time came for us to split a part. It always hurt me to see my baby cry and cry. She was crazy about her daddy but I was trying to make a better life for us. Things just were not looking up for me. He packed our belongings so he could get us back to Cleveland on time. I could see it in his eyes that he didn't want us to go back. He begged me to leave Zion with him and I could just go back but she was all I had. I wasn't going to make it without her. I needed her to be by my side; to give me that extra boost to continue on with life. We made it back down to the house. I couldn't go back in. I stood out waiting on my cousin to pull up so we could head to Memphis to catch our route to Atlanta Georgia.

Zion's dad stood there hugging and kissing his daughter as much as he could, embracing her, not knowing when the next time he would see her again. He grabbed my arm and said, "You know I love you, right?"

He gave me a hug and kissed me on my jaw. I didn't respond back I just smiled to keep from saying the evil things that were playing in my head. I didn't want to ruin the moment so even if it was a lie, I told him I loved him. But the difference between him and I, I meant what I said but not sure if he did. We waved goodbye as I got in the truck. I was torn. A part of me wanted to stay because of my daughter and part of me didn't. I was at the end of my rope struggling, pulling, and tussling trying to make it without support; without help. I always took everything to heart. Any little thing would have me stressed. Tears flowed and slowly I went into a silent killer of depression. On top of that, I still grieved the loss of my grandmother. My cousin asked if I was okay. I just smiled and told him I was fine. I was just tired. But all honesty, I was broken like a mirror shattered in a million pieces on the floor. I was toxic inside, empty and scarred deeply.

I hate traveling, all this riding and sitting was bothering me. I just want some sleep and some peace. We made it to the bus station in Memphis. Our bus was scheduled to leave at 1:15. We arrived before time so they tagged our luggage and assisted us on the bus. I set far back from everyone. I just wanted to be alone. I had zero tolerance plus we were about to have this long drive of hours on the road. I was determined to sleep the whole ride and to make sure I didn't have any interruptions, I cut my phone off. That didn't stop Zion from crying. She was hungry, and I fed her, soothing her until she was sound asleep. My queue to join her. I closed my eyes as well and suddenly began to dream:

"I'm walking along side an ocean, so peaceful so quiet, I feel a touch but don't see anyone. I jump because I am frightened, but the touch leaves and the effect on me left me speechless. The pain was gone, my heart was healed, and I could finally see things differently. It begins to rain, all of a sudden it storms. Suddenly, I run to get under a tree so I

61

wouldn't get wet, but as I step under the tree a big hole occupies the space. I fall, twisting and floating in a hole that never ends. I hear myself screaming in the dream and falling deeper and deeper as the hole gets larger"

One of the passengers shook me. I jumped, heart beating at a rapidly fast pace. The passenger had seen me fighting in my sleep as tears roll down my face. I sat pondering, trying to figure out what just happened to a dream that started so beautifully ended tragically. I closed my eyes, asking God what he was trying to tell me. He spoke to me just as plain saying, *Keep living, you will understand later.*

We made it to Atlanta safely. I was excited. I called Seven to get us from the bus station. She gladly did and said she missed us. The feeling was mutual. I wasn't sure how I was going to get through life after putting my grandmother down in the ground but I had a lot of soul searching, surrendering, and repenting to do. Taking one day at a time to get my life in order; to be on the right track.

Seven came in the computer room and we talked about how things went in Mississippi and about those bad boys that I was attracted to. I loved how I could always vent to her about anything. She would listen and if I was mad, she always made me laugh. More importantly, she gave me good advice. I was so grateful and thankful for our relationship.

Night came. My favorite time in Georgia was the ride to the city. I loved looking at those beautiful tall buildings and the lights were just beautiful. My heart was so excited. Before our ride was over, we stopped at the liquor store to get a bottle of Sutter Home, a drinking beverage of wine that

I absolutely fell in love with. It topped off our night along with our late-night sessions about life goals. It was so encouraging to hear about all the degrees and certificates she had accomplished throughout the years. Just hearing her story motivated me to finish what I started.

Life was hard for me, the fact that I ran from my problems made things worse but what amazed me about myself was how I was in a big city becoming attached to the fast life. I experienced a lot; I saw things so differently as I branched out from the small town in the "Delta". This challenged me to grow up. The transitioning of becoming the woman I needed to be vs. me transforming until someone I didn't know made it so difficult to cope with. I was fighting a battle and because of that, I couldn't move on and give God my life. I just wanted to flow through life without the pain and suffering, but in order to overcome this I knew I had to suck it up, move forward, healing the best I knew how.

Everything I faced was due to the decisions I had made based off my feelings, my emotions, and my way of thinking. I was self-centered, but in my heart, I was selfless, I would give anyone my last. My actions would speak for me whenever I did a good deed. I needed my heart and mind to be on one accord. Even though I wasn't living right, God still blessed me. Through my curse, He was actually calling me. I ignored the harkening of His voice every time He spoke. *I guess I will get it together sooner or later; I have to do better because I don't know how much time I have left on earth.* I fell asleep, mind overloaded. I was so caught up on my problems that I was blindsided that I was closing chapter 22 the next day.

By his grace, I woke up to a glorious morning. It was my birthday. I lived to see 23 years. Another year God allowed. It was the beginning of a new chapter, a new start, a clean slate, a blessing above anything that I was facing. Seven came to sing happy birthday to me, making my day extra special. As we prepared for the day, we went to Lenox Mall in Buckhead Georgia, shopped a little and ate plenty - had a wonderful time. Later on that night, we had a few friends over for drinks with the music blasting. I was on another planet. The drinks had me gone. I was feeling good, in my zone, vibing, moving to the beat, enjoying life. Who knows, the way God is calling me, this may be my last time living this lifestyle.

The next day I continued filling out applications and waiting on calls. I needed a job and I just wanted to finish school, getting my B.S. degree out the way. Every day went by, still nothing; weeks still nothing; a month absolutely nothing. I was like, *Lord what is it.* So I decided to call around. All positions were filled and the school that I desperately wanting to attend informed me with news I didn't want to hear, the administrator explain to me that I had all the requirements except one class. That one class caused me to miss getting accepted. That gave me a choice; either go back home to finish at Delta State or find a JUCO in Georgia. Just when I thought things were looking up for me, my breakthrough was still broken, and I needed to get through. Everything was going downhill. I contemplated going back home. I had moved to this big city and became stagnant. I didn't know which way to turn so my only thing to do was call on Jesus. Seek Him and pray. I was not sure if he would hear me, but I gave it a try because I needed guidance. Just when I thought he didn't hear me he spoke instantly telling me to move back home; I must finish what I started. I didn't obey. I stayed in Georgia for three more months still trying to make it work.

I tried but I was tired of trying to figure it out. I went online on the computer and bought a one-way ticket back to Mississippi. I didn't want to leave but my time was up. I tasted life and it was sour as can be in a big city with plenty of sweet opportunities and couldn't reach any of them because of my sinful ways and me disobeying God. He stopped me because I was in my mess. I didn't know who I was going to live with. My grandmother's house was no longer an option so I called my aunt and asked her if I could stay with her until I got on my feet. She agreed that I could. I had to suck it up and do it for my daughter. In due time. I guessed things would get right.

I thought I might as well enjoy the last week in Atlanta. Seven and I did something every day of the week until it was time for us to go. It was a bittersweet moment for me. I had gotten so close to these beautiful people, and my daughter and I had really grown to love them. We had a home away from home that we cherished and appreciated wholeheartedly. I knew if I was in any situation that caused me to be weighed down, I was always told I could come back whenever I was ready.

It was time to say goodbye to Georgia. I cried and cried as I really dreaded going back to Mississippi. I felt like I could have made it, at least I had hoped that I would. But all my blessings were blocked and on hold due to my disobedience, not heeding God's voice; going my own way. My life was already a disaster and if I get back, things may really turnout for the worse. The last thing I wanted to hear people say, "I told you, you couldn't make it in that big city. You're right back where you started."

I didn't have the energy for the negativity. I just wanted to be successful and great! I had enough of the hardships and pain. It was time for a major change. I was still trying to find my way. The pattern of lust, pain, and addiction had tried to ruin my life.

Sex Addict

Before I became a real sinner, I started out in life carefree. Even though I was born in sin, I was still happy. But as I got older and saw what life was truly about, it didn't take long for my views to change. It seemed like something was always coming against me. My life was headed down the wrong path, and my heart was shattered. I still decided to push and keep pushing forward. I needed to be somewhere in life but because of my unsteady ways, I couldn't move. I had done some things I wished I hadn't, and I was now reaping the consequences of it all.

What happened to me anyway? Life wasn't supposed to be this way. *God what happened? I'm not sure who I am.* "I'm glad you finally asked," God said. "I will take you back and show you where you went wrong and what your life would have been if you would have never ignored me when I was calling you to choose my way."

My heart ached as God showed me myself recalling all the things I did to get to this point of my life. The time came for me to face the responsibility of my decisions that I had been in denial about.

God said, "Do you remember when I told you to save yourself for marriage at the age of 19 and you lost your virginity. It made you feel terrible. I felt the guilt and shame but you wouldn't admit that you were wrong. You knew the Bible and went against it. I tried to stop you but it was too late. Your heart was already broken. Do you remember when you were revengeful to people who hurt you, causing more damage to yourself, tried to fix it and put me out of the whole situation?"

For me, life had become a performance and I realized that I had to *act* to be accepted. Deep in my heart, I knew things weren't right but I was too afraid to change. I was afraid of what my family or friends would think so I ignored God and drifted far away from Him in sin. I didn't want God to remind me. The more He did the more conviction came over me. All the time I felt that way, it was God calling me, but I didn't listen. I was so busy trying to do it my way, I didn't answer. He tried to get my attention during my storms, through my addictions, through my suffering. Only if I had listened it would have prevented so many heartaches that I cast upon myself. I was transitioning again, trying to fix my broken life so my aunt insisted that I talk to Prophet Henry. She thought it would help me see life in a different view. This was what I needed to see what my life truly was. I was lost and going through an identity crisis; I really didn't know which way to turn.

We met at his Church. He asked my name and instantly spoke in my life. All I could do was cry. Everything I was facing at that moment, I heard from God. My mouth was wide open because at that point, I was in awe. This man was all in my business. He knew nothing about me so I realized this was God. No doubt, it was Him, so I continued to listen. As Prophet Henry spoke, he said he could see me writing a book about poetry and that was my way of expressing how I felt. He also said he saw me writing another book that I'm unsure about. He proceeded to say he saw me moving to Florida, Texas, or Atlanta Georgia.

I was so excited as he continued to speak in my life saying, "I also see that God is going to bless you in the meantime with a job, a car, an apartment, and finishing school." He told me how courageous I was for being so strong and not weak minded to life. I filled up with so much emotion; all I could do was smile, cry, and embraced this wonderful man of God.

God showed me a vision of everything He had said. After leaving Prophet Henry, I had faith that I would make it despite what I was going through. Life seemed so much easier. I had heard from God and I knew all those things that were spoken would come to pass. After receiving that prophetic word, I anxiously waited to see God move on my behalf. The minute I left from Him, I went job searching, filling out job applications as well as apartment applications. Working my faith, whoever called first, I was willing to take the offer. As bad as it hurt, I didn't want to save money. I loved to spend but I knew what I was up against, so I saved every penny, only spending whenever necessary.

Finishing school was very heavy on my heart. I emailed my advisor and she graciously set up an appointment with me and gave me the date to register. I was so elated to see

God move so speedily. The following week before registering for school, I went to check on my application at KFC. My first talk with the hiring manager proved that more blessings were in my favor. She said she was about to call me because she needed me to fill out some paperwork, "We are in the process of making you a crew member for this corporation."

Not only would I be back in school, I'd be working too. To be honest, after moving back from Atlanta, Georgia, I didn't expect God to give me what I needed it right then and there. I was unsure about what he would do. As impatient as I was, I didn't think God would move so quickly. The doubt was real but at some point, I would gain patience and my trust would kick in too.

Things started to look up for me. The only area I was messed up in was Church (I wasn't quite back in Church yet) and sex was a major problem. While I gave the attention to the sex, I wasn't giving my all to God. I can honestly say I half stepped with Him. My relationship with Him was at its lowest as I really stayed away. I felt as if I only needed to grab Him when I wanted too. It wasn't fair. God had been so good to me but I treated Him as if He was a *nobody*. I made a vow to myself that I would start back paying my tithes and attending Church service. But I wanted to do it on my own time and not God's time.

The fact that I was living with my aunt mandated that we all go to Church. I just wasn't ready to follow that house rule. I knew what was set in my mind to do. I don't play with God so I moved at my own pace. At the same time, I didn't want to be forced either. I chose to go to Church whenever I was going through something and when I wasn't facing anything major. I would tough it out thinking I had figured it out but only swept it under the rug along with the rest of my problems. But mind you, I was sending my tithes to Church. Any money I gathered up, I gave it to God so I knew God would spare me; but for how long though. The way I was going, it didn't seem like God was even there.

I didn't have sex for the whole eight months I was in Georgia. I was amazed because I kept my body under control, but the minute I moved back… I think my addiction had spread into a disease called "STRONGHOLDS" because anybody that touched me I was ready to jump on top of them with no questions asked; craving for that pleasurable feeling that I knew wasn't good for me at all. It was so dangerous the way I was going. I was indeed whorish. I never did anything in broad day light. I was a night owl. I'm talking about the midnight hours early morning sun rising kind of creeping and not with just one man. I'd have two by the night and depending on how high my drive was for sex, I would call one more to get a quickie to finish off my high. Promiscuous at its best; extremely loose, wild and just messing up my life completely. I was different so I figured I need a different man for a different feeling. I just didn't care. I can admit that I was very selfish. I didn't think seriously about my daughter or my health. Just hopping from one man to the next. I could have contracted an STD or HIV. Did that stop me? No! I was trying to feel that feeling every day more often than not.

It wasn't love I was looking for. It was clear to me that it was only sex - nothing more nothing less. I chased after the lust to fill the empty void that I been trying to close. The whole time I was having sexual encounters with each man, my soul was tied to all of them. I was wrapped up in my feelings on a rollercoaster ride. I couldn't control it, so I tried to decide who I wanted to be with. But my soul wouldn't let me decide. Those lust demons took over my body completely. The addiction for sex grew stronger and stronger, and the way the men was sexing me, I couldn't resist either one. I kept having sex with all of them going back over and over. I asked myself why I kept doing this to my body. I knew it wasn't right, but the rush of pleasure that flowed through my body gave me the feeling I desired. It had thrilled me. I wanted to stop but the devil wasn't letting up. Every time I tried to call it quits, he convinced me that I wasn't through having fun. It had gotten so bad that I would masturbate while watching pornography. If I couldn't get the real deal when I wanted it, I had to add more fuel to the fire. It wasn't my main addiction, but it truly became a habit when I found out I could release pressure by pleasing myself. I ignored the men for a while. I found a new way. I needed help bad. Who was I turning into?

I wanted to do better. I tried to do better; and be better for my daughter. It was so hard I just wanted to stay focused while I took on the new journey; to work and go to school. I knew that the early mornings in class and the sleepless nights from work straight to homework would soon pay off. I knew God was not pleased with what I was doing. He convicted me every day I made a vow and didn't keep it. I got to the point where I neglected God with work and school and he was the one blessed me with what I needed. Sometimes I would pray here and there, barely read the word. I was a sinner trying to find her way through grace because mercy was not an option for me. I felt God's wrath. He dealt with me in ways I never expected.

My first fast food job. Did I like it? No! But because I knew where I stood. I had to work to defeat the odds that were trying to keep me down. Everything was such a rush, but I caught on, and before the week was out, I was running the front counter like I'd been there for months. When I worked, my mind was free. However, when I got off work, I was reminded where I was and didn't want to be. So to clear my mind, I would exercise or read a book; to have some sort of sanity. The school months came and went quick. I was half-way through the semester and made much progression on my job. I worried because God was blessing me with everything except one thing. No calls from any of the apartments I applied for. God spoke instantly saying to me, *My child be patient, stay focused.* I prayed and left it alone; I had something else to deal with. My daughter was not with me because there was not enough room at my aunt's house. Her dad and I made an agreement that she would be with him throughout the week and I'd have her on the weekends. I didn't like the idea at all but I had to do what was best for her so I could do things differently for us.

People talked down to me; calling me unfit, calling me a *poor excuse* for allowing my daughter to be out of my sight. It seemed as if no one liked what I was doing. It was clear that the ones who claimed they were happy for me were the ones mad at me. I didn't depend on them anymore, and it was more than enough fight left in me to finish this race I was running. Although they talked about me, my nonchalant attitude wouldn't let it get the best of me. It indeed made me stronger. I knew many people didn't believe in me. The people who I thought loved me, dogged me out. It was so terrible, I wanted to pack up again, but I knew leaving wouldn't solve anything. Besides, the outcome was speaking for itself; the work for me was in progress.

School was almost out so I contemplated on going to summer school to get ahead. I got the run down on what I needed before applying for graduation. I had eight classes left and I was able to take two over the summer. I took advantage of that offer. The less classes the closer to graduating, but more importantly to get my daughter back with me. I couldn't count how many times I cried myself to sleep and fell into a slump of depression. I felt as if everyone was against me, being that I didn't have much support or help. My daughter was all I had and her not being in my presence sucked the life out of me. I had to make myself focus and keep my head up because I knew greater was coming for us.

I went to work and before clocking in, I explained to the manager my new class schedule, hoping she could find some sort of rotation so I could still work and go to school. I felt myself breaking through my transition; chains breaking off me. Not having chains linked up to me and having what I needed to survive was a good thing. Getting off work, it was already late, and I was exhausted. Not only that, I had to go home to study for two tests and write a paper that had to be completed the next day. All I could do was ask God for his divine strength. Procrastination was not my cup of tea. My mind was racing and I was falling into anxiety attacks. You would have thought I'd commit suicide with everything I was facing. Did the thoughts roam through my head all the time?

However, I had to remind myself that I had a life beyond me. Every time I looked at her picture or called to talk to her, saved my life.

Before I started my assignments, I kneeled to pray. God came right in, clearing my mind. He made a way for me to stay focused and get everything completed. I didn't get much sleep and when I did drift off to sleep, my phone alarmed buzzed loudly in my ear. I had my morning session with God, was dressed, and headed out the door. I left early because I had to walk, but I ended up getting a ride. I was thankful for that. I gave God the first fruits of my day and he took care of me right in the midst. I tried to keep my mind off everything. It was test day, but my mind fell on sex. I had not engaged in sex in a while, so I knew the devil would come for me sooner or later. I asked God to drive them thoughts away. I knew it was nobody but the enemy trying to distract me.

As I got ready to test, my phone was vibrating constantly. It kept ringing and beeping, and I'm wondering who this could be calling like this. I stepped out to go to the restroom. I had text messages from two guys, both asking to see me. I knew sex was all they wanted so I didn't respond back. My attention was on the unfamiliar number that had called several times. I called back. No answer. I went back to finish taking my test when the phone ring again. I answered it in the middle of testing. The voice on the other end said, "Hi. Miss Howze? I was calling to let you know we have an apartment available for you."

I screamed a loud *THANK YOU JESUS*. Not knowing when God told me to leave it alone, he was working it out. I was so joyful inside. *I'm employed, I have income, I'm a senior in college, months away from getting my B.S. in social work, and now I have my own set of keys - To my place.*

The more God did for me, the more I doubted Him. Sounds crazy, right? I know, you would think the trust would excel. No, I worried a lot, over analyzed everything a tad bit too much, and I still wasn't satisfied. My depression increased. That joy didn't last too long. I had all the necessities but still wasn't happy. I still felt empty inside, but I kept pressing on. Even on thin ice, God was with me, and he made sure I got through life.

As summer school approached, working and trying to remove the stress was taking over my body. I needed a release fast, and because the devil knew my weakness it didn't take him long to be slick. Marlow wrote to me on Facebook. I kept saying, NO! I'm going to let him be but I was so stressed I fell into the temptation. I called him back and of course, he asked if I wanted to go half on a hotel room. I told him I couldn't because I would soon be moving into my own place. So he purchased the hotel himself. Lord knows I didn't need to be doing this. I had work stacked over my head and had just gotten off work. But, before going to the library, I went to the hotel instead.

Marlow wanted to talk but I didn't. I became really aggressive with him. In all honesty, I had missed how he sexed me. It was long overdue. I couldn't keep my self-control, and the sexual encounter began. Now I am right back in the same place I didn't want to be. After getting pleasured and the tension off me, I can admit it felt so good but for how long. It would be hard for me to leave him alone once again. After we finished, he wanted me to stay because he didn't have to work but I knew I couldn't. He insisted that he would drop me back off at home, but I told him to take me to the library where I was supposed to have been to begin with. I felt bad, I felt uneasy, and it was a Church night. I know God wasn't please; I had fallen short of his glory, again. Broke my vow so I know I would have to pay for every sin I committed.

This man (Marlow) didn't want any part of me. I fell again for his sweet nothings and pillow talk so I said my typical prayer when I always did wrong, *Lord please forgive me. I won't do it again. I'm trying, it's hard.* I thought, *God has turned his back on me; he heard me, but he was not in a place of pleading with me.*

He spoke back saying, *It's my turn now,* so at this point I knew he was about to make me go through the trenches.

I called KFC to get my schedule. I didn't have to work that next day so after class I was able to start moving into my new place. I called my cousin to see if he would help me move and he said yes. I moved as much as I could in so my daughter and I could move in soon. My aunt called and asked if I would be able to help with grocery for the month. I told her I couldn't. I had to make grocery for my new place. She was surprised, saying she didn't know I was moving. In reality, no one knew. I moved in silence. I was paying attention to the hints that were thrown. My aunt replied, *Yeah, grown people need their own place.*

I couldn't have agreed more. I hung up the phone and did some finishing touches around my apartment before I left. The minute I hung up my phone rang again. It was Marlow asking about a repeat of Thursday night. I didn't turn it down.

I went home, freshened up, got pretty (only to feel empty afterwards), and rented a hotel room. This time I paid for it.

Marlow said he wanted a baby by me. I'm like, *No way. I'm having a hard time now plus you don't want to settle down.* He tried his hardest not to wear a condom but I couldn't go with that. **No Glove No Love** or we don't have to have sex at all. He put the condom on.

During sex, he was whispering in my ear saying he can't stop messing with me, he doesn't want to leave me alone. I said *well put a ring on it.* I'm lying there while he is stroking every move and I clearly hear God say, *What you are doing is wrong. Get up and leave now.*

I pushed Marlowe off of me, crying and yelling at him, *Take me home now. I can't do it anymore. You don't love me. You're just using me.*

He starts talking, calming me down, kissing all over me and the next thing I know, we're having sex again. I wanted out when we finished.

My heart was so heavy, I was convicted, I was torn, and I was hurt. The pain was killing me softly. I had disobeyed God. He had told me to leave but I insisted on feeding my lustful desire. This addiction was getting out of hand. I told God I was tired. The sex demons were on the loose. It seemed like I couldn't stop. Then porn became an addiction. I was always horny with hormones raging out of control and if I couldn't get pleased, I would do the honor of pleasing myself. And if that wasn't enough, I would have phone sex. I had somebody I could call anytime I wanted to add a boost to my feelings. It got crazy; things got out of hand. This stronghold not only took over my body, but my life too.

I went to work that morning. I was drained mentally and physically. Sex three days in the row. Who wouldn't be tired? I had no energy; none whatsoever. I had to force myself to work. It got so busy in there and this time I didn't have help. We were short on cashiers, not only was I working the front counter I was doing drive thru as well. I'm taking orders and packing at the same time. The head boss walks in asking why the line was backed up. I explained to him that I was running both counters front and drive thru and I'm only one person. I had to get the job done because one of the cashiers did *a no call, a no show*, so he took over drive-thru while I attended to the front. The orders backed up on the line and he was screaming, going into an uproar asking me why I am moving so slow. But that was never the case. I still didn't have help in the front so I had to take my time so I wouldn't mess any one's orders up. It was no secret how he embarrassed me in front of my co-workers and customers. But being a humbled person, I just walked off; didn't say a word. He told me to clock out for the rest of the day. Then he said as a matter-of-fact give me my shirt and hat. I gave it to him and I left, walking home. I'm crying I'm pleading to God because I have lost my job, my rent was coming up that following week, and my light bill was already due. I had to get an extension until I could get some help. Now I have to get help with rent too.

God really got my attention. I cried and prayed for three days because I needed a miracle to fall fresh down on me. My mind was all over the place. My faith had to be put into action. I didn't know how this was going to play out to ease my mind. I would always walk my daughter to the park. This time, we didn't go the park, we went to Church right down the street. Attending bible class and hearing the Word was just for me. I will never forget the message as it was said: "You can't serve two masters. You either with God or with the devil. Which one would you choose? In my head I'm like, *Okay Skyye, it's time to answer this calling. I'm tugging war with my life. I'm a queen for the devil but I want God more than anything because that's the only way I can live fully. I just don't know what to do at this point. I don't want to keep doing wrong.*

God always made way for me even though my life was under a massive curse. We walked back to the house, and two guys were standing outside. One approached me saying how beautiful I was and how he had been watching me since I moved over there.

I said, "Okay! Your point?" It was typical of me to get smart; I had a smart mouth.

So the guy proceeded to say, "I got to have you."

"Oh yeah?"

He said, "Yes."

I laughed and walked into my apartment.

Now I think I'm being tested with the guy who approached me. I was in a place where I'm trying to transition from listening to my favorite rappers, Lil Boosie and Lil Wayne, and my favorite R&B singer Chris Brown. I was truly a fan of these men. Every album they came out with, I had it, but I wanted to try something new. Plus, I had made up in my mind, I think… to do right and do things Gods way. Although I loved all genres of music, I had a thing for hardcore rap. As sweet and soft as I am, I was kind of rough when it came down to rap music. I was cleaning up my apartment and playing a gospel song called *Give Me You* by Shana Wilson. That song broke me down. My spirit was lifted. My body was calm. I was in a place where I needed God more than anything. That song spoke to me in various ways. I continued to listen to the music, and I'm like *Lord, I can't seem to grasp this.* As soon as the gospel song ended, I was back playing Lil Boosie. I had the whole album on my phone. The song I played every day was *Devil Get Off Me,* failing to realize that the devil was the reason why I was in this shape. I continuously fell in his traps, being foolish as I could be. It was so hard for me. I had school, and I didn't have anyone to keep my daughter, so I allowed my mother to stay with us to help. I didn't want her on the streets anymore, so it was beneficial to me and her, so I thought.

Zion and I were getting ready for bed when a knock on my door startled me. It was the guy who had approached me earlier. I asked, "Who is it?"

"Jaden."

I didn't open the door.

"Come outside."

I said, "No! I got to get up early for school tomorrow."

He insisted on coming back the next day.

I said, "Yeah, whatever." And I walked away from the door to get me some sleep. I tossed and turned all night. I knew it was God dealing with me. Even though I was in my mess that never kept me from *trying* to keep God first before. I would do anything concerning my daughter, myself, or anybody else. I made sure I gave Him the first part of my morning. I began to read my Bible in the book of Genesis on how the snake convinced Eve to eat that forbidden fruit. And how she then tempted Adam to eat it as well! Just from that situation along it was much deception and temptation. God spoke to me telling me that I would be tricked out of some things and I would be tempted but do not go astray. I had to stay focused on what was spoken in my life. Guess what? I didn't listen. I did what I wanted to do, and because of that, the turmoil began. Again.

I drifted off to sleep, waking up to my daughter kissing on my face. I always loved how she was my personal alarm clock. I got ready for school, as Zion lay down peaceful, getting more sleep. My mom called me in the living room, "Skyye, don't you dare give up. You are way too smart. You can do it."

Heading out the door, I told my mom I loved her, while thinking of a shortcut to get to school faster. That way, I wouldn't have to get up so early or worry about being late. I'm walking and listening to music to soothe my mind, letting my mom's words stimulate my heart. I tried to stay focused, but worried at the same time. I didn't know if we would be in a hotel or homeless. The rent due date was getting closer and closer. The more I thought on it, the more I stressed. I didn't have income coming in anymore, and my mom never had it to begin with. Lord, what am I going to do? I made it to class, settled in, held my head down, and said a little prayer to clear my mind. School was getting the best of me. With so much overwhelming work, I didn't know if I was coming or going. *God, I need you like now.* The suicidal thoughts were playing hard in my head. With God's grace, I made it through the day. Before I knew it, school was over.

On my way home, I saw Jaden. He told me to get in the car so he could take me home and asked what I had planned for the weekend.

"Minding my business."

"I'm coming over to spend some time with you."

I said, "Humph I'll think about it."

The conversation ended as I thanked him for being a gentleman, giving me a ride home.

"No problem," he said as he pulled away.

I enter the house and *no signs of my mom or daughter.* I had been looking forward to seeing my daughter. My day was rough, and she was always the highlight of my day. I called to find out their whereabouts. My mom they would be home later. That gave me time to contact someone at Community Action. They set my appointment for 1:00 p.m. the next day. I gathered up all my documents. I was in desperate need of help for my rent and light bill.

I walked outside and here comes Jaden. I'm like, "Give me a break please. Why are you bothering me, dude?"

He said, "I can't. You so beautiful to me. I just want to look in your face."

I'm saying in my head, *The shape I'm in, I can't stand to look in my own face, let along someone else face.*

My daughter's dad called trying to see when he could pick up Zion. Without any hesitation, he mentions sex; saying he missed it. He wanted to taste me and everything else. I'm like don't you have a girlfriend?

He said, "So. I want you."

I'm shaking my head, not responding back to his statement, but bringing up what I had gathered up money-wise for rent. I explained to him how I needed to make ends meet. He brought the money the next day. In fact, he gave me half of what I needed, bringing it to me on campus after class.

I left for my appointment soon after so I wouldn't be late. I was extremely tired. I asked God for strength the whole time as I walked trying to get where I needed to be. I finally made it to the Community Action office and my name was called as soon as I walked in the door. I gave the lady my paperwork and she made a copy of everything. She said, "Miss Howze I haven't received your application."

And I know I gave her everything because I double-checked twice. I said are you sure? She said I have nothing you will have to come back in the morning I just smiled and walked off. All I could think about was how my lights would be off the next day, plus I had to study for a test. I called my instructor and she said I could make it up that next week. That gave me enough time to study some more.

I received an unknown call. I picked up the phone and it was Marlow. I had blocked him on my phone. He claimed he missed me. I said, "Marlow, if sex is what you want, you will have to up some rent money. So what's up?"

He hung up, (LOL). I texted Jaden to see what he was doing. He tried to come over. I wouldn't let him. He popped up anyway, knocking on my door like he was crazy. I said, "What do you want from me?"

"It's you I want. I'm so attracted to you."

"Well, my pockets need to attract some money. My rent is coming up." He claimed he would see what he could do to help. He left because he was mad that I didn't want to spend time with him!

The temptation was rising high now. I pondered, *should I have sex with Zion daddy, Jaden or Marlow*? Then I said, "No." I left all of that alone, but then again my rent was due. I had no other choice. I was left hanging. I called around for help; couldn't get it. Although my thoughts were wrong, I asked God to forgive me because He knew what I was going to do before I did it. And the way things were looking, it was either the streets or a hotel. I couldn't risk letting my daughter down nor getting her taken away from me. So, I prepared for the weekend. Zion would be gone, which gave me plenty of time to move around. It was also my birthday weekend. I was turning 24, but my birthday wasn't my focus, only my bills. I left the house to walk; get some fresh air. Jaden pulled up making demands, telling me he would be over that night. I just looked at him. My phone rings. It was Zion's granny telling me her uncle was coming to get her. I had to turn around go home to get her bag ready. While waiting for them, Zion came in the door hugging and kissing on me. My aunt also stopped by to see if I was going to Church. I said yeah, I would go since I hadn't been in a long time. I left; for what reason, I don't know. I didn't know how I would feel, what would they think? But I still went; Zion's ride pulled up, I kissed her telling her I loved her, as she settled in the car.

I had a long day ahead of me so I decided to take a nap, but I forgot I promised my aunt I would go to Church with her. I walked around to her house to catch them before they left. The whole time riding there, I felt uneasy and unnerved not knowing what to expect. But when I entered the Church, everyone seemed happy to see me. I was in my mess and didn't think it was a good ideal to visit Church because I was so far off from God, still trying to find my way. I was ready to leave the minute I hit the door! I knew God wasn't pleased with me. I felt it, and it didn't feel good. Besides, I had other plans I needed to handle. This needed to be over so I can get my money up was what I was thinking. I couldn't allow my family to be in the dark or on the streets.

Church was finally over. On my way back to my apartment, I was into deep thoughts asking myself why life was so hard. God said, *You are the reason why life is hard. Your pride and ego won't let you be submissive to me. When you do things your way it will always fail you. Do it my way and you will have favor.*

I went in the house, laid across the bed, reading a book, trying to relax my mind. Someone interrupted my rest with a knock on the door. It was Jaden telling me to let him in. I opened the door. He said he wanted to talk. Leading him back to my bedroom where I was reading, he asked how my day was and what I was reading.

"I see you like reading," he said.

"I do. In fact, I love to read. So, what's up with you. How was your day, Jaden?"

He said, "I have a confession."

"Proceed," I said softly.

"I have a family."

I already knew this. My observation led me to everything I needed to know about him. I said, "That's cool. You aint my man and if you cared so much about your family why are you here at the present?"

"I like how you listen to me, how we vibe. I can talk to you about anything without an argument taking place."

I already knew what he wanted. I was just waiting on him to make his move. He went to my door and locked it. I said, "Ummhh! Sir, what are you doing?"

"I want to make love to you like you never had it before."

He started kissing on me, got to rubbing me, and I'm pushing his hands back. He grabbed me, aggressively threw me on my stomach, rubbing between my legs until I gave in. He made his way inside of me. The heat of the moment ruined my life. Again. Within a few minutes, he ejaculated in me. It happened so fast, I'm sitting there like *what just happened?* I had enough problems. I instantly made him go home; I was so angry with him. With myself.

I fell asleep angry, waking up to my phone alarm. It was 6:00 in the morning. I jumped up so I could get to Community Action. The place wasn't opening until 8:00 a.m. but I had to be there. I needed help. I grabbed something to snack on and headed out the door. I took my time walking - to kill time. When I arrived there, a woman was sitting in front of the door. I'm friendly so I asked how she was doing, sparking up random conversation. The owner pulled up, opened the door, but before sitting down, I went up to the desk to sign in. I explained what took place before. I let her know that the lady I had spoken to before told me to come back in the morning because my application had been misplaced. God planted my eyes on the garbage can beside the copying machine. My application was in there –ripped. The lady from the day before came out. I looked at her with the application and smiled. She changed her attitude saying, "Don't worry, Miss Howze. Your light bill is going to get paid."

She knew what she did was wrong. I could tell she felt bad because she got caught. I waited in the office four hours. My bill was paid about noon, and I was still able to make it to my last two classes. I couldn't do anything but thank God. *Now I have to make plans to get the rest of my rent money up!*

I picked up my phone to check my TL on Facebook and discovered that one of my family members passed away. I'm like. *Lord, now this?* I'm barely living and here comes something else that was so heavy on my heart. It seemed like the pain just wouldn't go away. I was trying to do right. Where was I going wrong? Then I thought about the message in Church. It's either God or the devil. I'm fighting trying to pick who I will live for. Those strongholds were taking over me. The more I was tempted, the more temptation came my way. I needed the devil to stop riding me because I was minutes away from killing myself.

My aunt from Memphis wrote me in my inbox telling me she would be down sometime that week. She wanted to see the baby and me. I was excited. We didn't see one another much so I was looking forward to that sweet visit. I caught a sharp pain in my side that caused me to lie down. I felt a headache that form within seconds. My ear started throbbing. A sickness came over my body fast. Everything was coming against me. I closed myself in my room; shut my eyes until I drifted off to sleep. I dreamed:

"A big white van came up beside me, opened the door, snatched me up, throwing me inside. Somehow, I ended up in a dark alley. So many sexual things were taking place with no escape. I got tired and I broke away. I ran trying to ask

for help. The man shot me in the arm, dragging me by my hair while the blood ran deeply from my arm. He made me sign a contract that read, "If I refuse to give my body up to anyone, they will kill me.""

My phone rang. I jump, sweat pouring off me like water. I was shaking because God was trying to get my attention. But once again, I ignored the dream. Maybe this dream meant I should leave Jaden alone. I had started to catch feelings for him, and it was time to cut him off completely.

It was him calling, interrupting my dream. What a coincidence. I didn't answer.

Phone rings again. It's my "new friend" asking me if I was hungry. I said yes. He came to pick me up and we went out to eat. I received a text message from Zion's dad asking if he could come over later that night. I told him, yeah, but he would have to wait until I came home from the party that I was going to go to later with my friend, Casey. She had asked me early in the week to go with her. He said, "Cool. Let me know."

I'm enjoying this new guy. He seemed chilled. He was very nice to me. I asked him if he could pay my phone bill. He said he would without wanting anything in return. But I knew that was a lie. He turned right around and said what you going to give me. I'm saying to myself, I just met him, I don't plan on giving it up that fast, and not tonight either because my agenda was already full.

We left the restaurant going back to my place when he said, "When you ready for the money, call and let me know.

I will bring it to you." He flaunted it in my face, "I have the money right here,"

I got out of the car, calling Casey to see if she was still going to the party.

She said, "Yes."

"I'm still interested in going."

Getting ready to enter the shower, I heard loud knocks pounding on my door. My phone was ringing off the hook at the same time. I slipped something on to open the door and there stood Jaden pushing, opening, and slamming my door as if he paid bills there.

He went into a rage, "So you F**king another nigga and what the F**k that nigga doing down here coming out of your apartment."

I laughed because the last time I checked, I was single, while he had a whole family at home. I was a tab bit confused.

He stared at me and said, "You glowing. Are you pregnant?"

"No! Please leave me alone. I'm trying to get ready for a party."

I took my shower and got dressed. Jaden ranted some more telling me he loved me, and he didn't want to see me with anyone else. Followed up with the question, "Can I come over tonight?

"No, you can't, Jaden. I got something to handle."

"The only thing you need to be handling is making love to me. I been craving for you."

I said, "Oh well. Too bad."

Casey sent me a text message. She was outside. I pushed Jaden out the door and locked up my apartment. I was happy to see my best friend. Life had been a disaster and all that I was facing. Getting out of the house was all I needed.

Riding to the party, we talked and caught up, especially about men. Men were always our favorite topic of conversation. Enjoying our time together all while Zion's dad was blowing up my phone. I finally answered and he started questioning me like I was his woman. I told him not to ask about my whereabouts. He said he was in town.

I'm like, "Ok! You will just have to sit and wait until I'm finished."

I felt sick the moment I walked into the party. *Now here goes my Mama calling saying she was locked out and she had lost the key.* I'm like damn I'm trying to enjoy myself. I told Casey I had to leave the party because my mom was locked out. I knew she didn't want me to leave or be there by herself but my mom couldn't find me a ride so Casey had to take me home.

My night was messed up. I went home, sat and waited for my mom. She rushed me home and never showed up. I called Zion's dad to let him know to be on his way because I was at home. He was knocking on the door in no time. I'm guessing he was already outside. We went into my room, started making out, and he ripped off my clothes. As we were engaged in having sex, I heard a knock on my window. It was Jaden. I didn't stop riding. It felt too good to stop. My phone rang. It was my mom. At that point, we had switched positions, I was bent over. I didn't answer for her either. I was too busy trying to throw it back. We took a break. Somebody knocked on the door again.

I'm like, "OMG, who is this now?"

This time, it was my mom telling me she'd been calling me on my phone. I went back to my room. Zion's dad and I lay there talking and before I knew it, we were at it again and again and again. After we finished, I fell sound asleep. I don't even recall him leaving. I woke up trying to figure out should I go to Church or not. I laid there looking at the ceiling until I fell back to sleep.

I'm a light sleeper so I heard someone tipping by my room door. It was my aunt from Memphis. I was so happy to see her. She hugged me, kissed me on the forehead, and asked about Zion. In fact, Zion was on her way back to the house. She waited around so she could treat Zion to McDonalds. While sitting there, she asked, "How is life treating you?"

"I'm here, I'm blessed, and I'm almost finished with my BS degree. I'm looking for a job so I can have some income."

She encouraged me saying, "God will make a way. He's not going to leave you in this situation long."

My soul was refreshed.

She said, "Here is $16. I want to bless you with this before I get back on the road."

Zion didn't make it back in time, but before she headed out, she got us something to eat. I was so thankful for her. We said our goodbyes as she was driving off. I didn't go to church after all, but I said I would go to bible class on Wednesday since I missed service. I also decided to fast for that whole week. We were low on groceries; I was willing to do that so my daughter could eat. I could see God working on me. I was stretching.

Those growing pains hurt but I needed a change. My heart was tired of the same thing. Now the plan was to fast not only from foods, but also from men, sex and anything that was causing a distraction with my relationship with God. The minute my new friend called, I changed my mind. I needed that money to pay my phone bill. He wanted to know if he could swing by. He said that he would stop by after he got out of class.

I'm sitting doing my homework, Marlow calling asking if he can come over. I told him give me two weeks. He claimed he wanted to make up from being away. I said yeah ok whatever. I returned to doing my work. The new guy comes, and he has food in his hand so guess what? That fast with the food came to an end real fast. We sat around talking. I lay on his chest drifting into the smell of his cologne. He kissed me on the neck. One thing led to another, and we slipped into having sex. Besides, I needed the money, and as soon as we finished, he put the money in my hand. I had hustled up $600 within four days. Not only did I have both the rent and my phone bill paid, I had extra left over, which went to my daughter's needs. I didn't care about going without, I had to provide, and by any means necessary, I did exactly that.

I was in deep though and I felt awful because I let God down once again. I'd made vows and more vows but not living through them. God was really dealing with me. I was blessed but cursed too. I just wanted to get out of this war. I was tired of fighting it and tired of not doing things pleasing to God. I wanted to make God proud and make my daughter proud, but I was so complacent with the stronghold of addiction. *How must I go on Lord? I need your help.*

I thought about all the foolish things I did within four days to get money. Desperate times calls for desperate measures and I was in desperate need. I was so tired from having sex I just wanted to sleep my life away but unfortunately studious was all I could be. I had a test to make up. I sat up for more than two hours storing information in my head so I could pass my test. I'm not a last-minute person but because responsibility called, I had to do what I had to.

In most cases, school was my heart's desire but if I had to put it on hold again, I would, just so my family could survive. I laid down feeling sick. Suddenly, my body was shutting down on me. I began to breathe heavily. I was lying there unable say a thing. The pain was unbearable. All I could do was cry. I couldn't find the Medicaid card. I had to order another just to see the doctor. Luckily, I found some pain pills. It helped to remove the pain for a moment. I prayed hard and I felt God drift away; no signs no wonders I felt in my heart my prayer was truly in vain. I needed God. I know I disobeyed Him, and I suffered through all the pain.

I cried myself to sleep, waking up to a phone full of chaos, mess, and drama that I clearly didn't have time for. I overlooked all that because I had to prepare myself for my test. Mind you, I'm still feeling ill, but I walked on to school anyway. *I'm across the stage. Can't stop here.*

After I finished taking the test, I went to the library to check my grades. The joy to see that I was passing all my classes made my heart smile. Through all the distractions, the pain, the tests, and the trials, I remained a humble person and focused on school. I let nothing steal my drive. I let nothing or no one decide my determination. I let no one underestimate my devotion to my dreams and goals. I was going through hell and the devil was helping me; trying to kill me mentally. Somehow, my brainpowers fought and bounce back often. I fall. I get right back up. I fail at anything, I try until I succeed. I lose faith; I gain it right back with the word of God. I always believed in holding God, my child's dreams, and goals, dearest to my heart. I pushed with no limits with those three. The money my aunt gave me set heavy on my heart. God spoke to me telling me to put the $16 in Church. I said Lord that's all I have he said do you trust me? I said I do. Sometimes I'm more worried than anything. He said I need you to obey and watch the miracle that's about to happen on your behalf. And to think I was about to get something to eat. My mom, my daughter, and I went to bible class, sitting attentive, listening to the word and the topic was *Do You Believe?*

The message was confirmation from when God spoke to me earlier. I asked for the tithe envelope. Here comes the devil whispering just put $10 in and keep six. I almost compromised with the devil but I obeyed God, sealed the whole $16 and let my daughter put it in the tray as they passed it around. It felt so good. My spirit shifted, my mind was clear. I could feel God's presence all over me. No matter if I was in Church or out of Church, I always believed in keeping God first and paying my tithes. Someday I knew I would reap the benefits of a harvest that eyes haven't seen, and ears haven't heard.

Marlow texted me saying he bought me red lingerie and that he wanted me to wear for him. I told him I would see him soon, I'm still recouping from feeling sick. All that sexing I was doing I needed my body to recover. His birthday was coming up. I knew I didn't need to be doing this, but I knew for a fact he would set the money out just because it was me. Sometimes it doesn't have to be because of sex.

We stop texting and I used my phone to fill out job applications and checked on the old ones I filled out when I first moved back from Georgia. I was still in a bind; the next month's rent was approaching. My mom wasn't helping at all, so I figured she was leeching off me. I was angry. I tried to help her, and she was using me. Not to mention she lied when I asked her about getting SNAP. She said she didn't receive any, but I found a letter where she had already recertified for that previous month. I'm guessing the drug man had her card and that's how she paid for her drugs. Things started to add up. I forgave her and I still let her stay with me even with her addiction. We both had strongholds. I was fighting trying to get rid of mine while she continued to feed hers.

Marlow came by. He said, "Skyye, I been wanting to ask you this, but I was afraid, and I know how crazy you can get, and you possibly will stop having sex with me."

"What is it?"

"I want to have a threesome with you."

Now I never stooped this low, but I needed some money. I said, "As long as you got $700 up front, I'll do whatever you want me to do." I asked if it would be with a man or woman.

"A woman."

Now this was my chance to be in a bed with another woman. Something I'd always been curious about. This was my opportunity to really explore what my mind been wondering about for so long. I'd never been attracted to women. It always had been the opposite for me with women. Lesbians, to be exact, had always come on to me. I guess they sensed the curious side of me wanting to be involved with a woman. I needed my pleasure to go up another level anyway, and I thought this would do it or turn me out to be gay.

My phone rang and disturbed our conversation. It was Prophet Henry calling to check on me. He told me I was very heavy in his spirit, asking was everything okay? All I could do was cry because of what I was going through. I stepped out the room away from Marlow to explain to Prophet Henry how I had lost my job but still pressing my way through school. I told him I was on the verge of losing my apartment, and the suicidal thoughts were coming at me fast. I said, "I'm struggling with this addiction of having sex every time I meet a man."

He stopped talking and began to pray for me right then and there. After he finished praying, he was telling me that Church's Chicken was hiring and to fill out an application. I had one on file already from about two years ago. He insisted that I call as soon as we hang up, so I did. The general manager found my application. She told me to give her about a week to call back. I was so excited all I could think about is how I planted that $16 seed and in less than three days, a miracle came my way.

I could never understand why God blessed me the way he did. I was a professional sinner living off his grace, working for the devil full time. But God said, *Although you disobey me with your body, your heart always obeys when it's time to give. You put others needs before your own, else especially in my temple you are very obedient in that area.*

My mind was blown at this point. I just experienced again what God can do. *Look at God* was all I could say. Everything was starting to fall into place, but my life was still under brokenness, full of chaos, and my spirit was not where it needed to be.

So, Marlow says let's go to the Hotel so we can get started on this threesome. I didn't make it out the door good before the pain in the bottom of my stomach started hurting so bad until I couldn't move. He helped me to a chair where I sat down. He asked if I was okay. I said no and told him I couldn't go with him. He was mad. I didn't care. When he left, I decided to make a doctor's appointment. But the pains became sharper and sharper so I'm like I can't wait. I started walking to the OB-GYN. This was unusual for me. The more I walked, the more I had to push through those pains with every step I made. I finally arrived at the office and told them what I was going through. The nurse called for my doctor and he got me in an examining room at once. He checked my cervix area; the part I hated, but I lay uncomfortable with my legs spread wide open as he examined. He talked and joked with me to get my mind off the pain. After he finished probing me, I put my clothes back on and met him in his office. He said he didn't see what was causing the sharp pains, everything came back negative. I'm saying to myself I was having sex with different men and unprotected at that. No STDs, No HIV. All test results were very much normal. I knew this was God sparing me, I knew it was Him protecting me from diseases. I couldn't stop thanking God. It was Him who healed my body. When I left that doctor's office, all my pain was gone.

When I arrived back at my apartment, I saw my landlord posting a paper on my door. He saw me and said he needed to talk to me. I asked him what about?

"Have you found a job yet?"

I said, "My application was pulled but no interview yet."

"Well, Ms. Howze if you don't have your rent at the end of the week, you have 16 days to pack up and be removed from my property."

I had $160 but he wouldn't take it. He needed me to pay the whole thing. I already knew I wasn't going to have it by then, so I had to start looking for a place to stay. I was confused and frustrated, and had no help, but I trusted God. I knew this was yet another test. Walking down the street, I was led to go into my old apartment building where I lived when I was 20 years old. My very first apartment. The manager was getting ready to leave the property, and before he could back out, I stopped and asked him if he had anything available for rent.

He said, "I have a one bed room available with first month rent and deposit. It will be $800."

"Sir, I don't have that type of money."

"Give me what you have. Since it's the end of the month and we can go from there."

I gave him the $160. He wanted me to *just* add $40 to it to make it $200 even.

God was working that $16 I sowed in Church. The devil wanted me to call Marlow for the rest of the money and God wanted me to seek help from the Church. I did the right thing and they gave me $150. Just when I thought God forgot about me, even when I gave up on myself, He was still there turning it around for me. I took him the rest of the money he gave me my key. I left from there and went straight to class. I didn't eat anything but I was so full off what God was doing, I didn't want to eat. I fasted all that day. I was tempted from the smell of food, so instead of me going to the Union or the Café, I went to the library to stay ahead on my assignments. I started on one of my papers and my phone started to vibrate. I didn't know the number, so I hesitated, but I answered it.

Hello, is this Skyye?

Yes, this is she.

Can you come in for an interview at 10:30 tomorrow morning?

Yes ma'am. I had class but I didn't mind skipping just that one class. I had to get things done so I could support my family. I went into the rest room thanking God as the tears of joy fell. The move of God was really manifested in my sinful life. The favor was still strong upon my life. My faith was up and down but through it all, I maintained and came through to new beginnings. My relationship with God was taking its course, flowing in the right direction. If He just continued to hold my hand, I was sure I'd be everything He was calling me to be.

Miracle Delivery

Until that 16th day, we stayed in the old apartment packing up everything while I continued attending my classes. During all of it, I had made it through the interview process, drug tested, and a physical before the on-the-job training began. It was indeed stressful. I sat down with my mom, and as pleasant as possible, let her know that she could no longer live with us. Of course, she was angry, but I didn't want to continue taking care of someone who didn't want to help herself. Yes, she helped me watch my little girl, but all the time I didn't feel safe. I knew what she was capable of doing. Besides, I needed a sound and peaceful mind for what lie ahead. It wasn't enough room anyway, and too much for me to bear at that moment. She was so furious with me, she stopped helping me pack. My depression kicked in again. I went into a weary stage - mind going completely black, crying, wanting to be shut up in a dark place; to hear only silence so I could be alone; to pull strands of hair out, as my brain went numb from the things I dealt with daily.

This new transitioning took its toll on me. I felt empty inside. I had temporarily refrained from fulfilling my passion. Now this void had caused my body to go through withdrawals – from pleasure and wanting. I had decided to stop having sex; tried to do things God's way. Still my flesh craved that lustful desire to continue, while my spirit wanted to abstain and be free from fornication. I even changed my number. I was very serious about keeping my walk on track with God.

God had blessed me with a job and another place to live so I was willing to obey Him. I cut everybody off so my blessings would continue to flow properly. Since Mom would no longer be with us, I had to search for a daycare. Meanwhile, Zion's other family took care of her on the days I worked, and I was very much thankful for that.

Moving was so tiresome, but I had to transport as much as I could into my new apartment before getting dressed for work. But as God would have it, on my way to work, I looked up and saw a daycare. I walked into the building and spoke to the woman sitting in the office. I informed her that I was looking for childcare. She gave me an application and I filled it out on the spot. She told me to bring the rest of the information back and we would go from there. I left and headed on to work. As I walked, I was in deep thought. *I'm at my breaking point with walking everywhere. I didn't have transportation, and no one would give me a ride unless I had gas money. I was ready to escape this despair.*

I made it in the door at my exact time, clocked in, and began my workday. I loved to work. It kept my mind off a lot of stuff. Although I'm a friendly person, at the same time, I'm an observer. I always watched my surroundings. Of course, I talked to everyone, but there were many I was cautious with. Drama and mess. I despised it. Life was already throwing bricks at me but God still blessed me in spite of the obstacles I faced. Being involved in drama was a no-go for me so it was vital that I stayed to myself. I didn't have the time or the energy. Even though God blessed me, I still had trials and tribulations that were certainly out of my control.

I had training/orientation on the computer before working the floor. After the boss showed me around, with all the things I had to do, she said I could go home and pick up where I left off the next day. It was a pretty long day. I couldn't wait to get home. As I walked out the door, I was so dizzy, I almost fell. I had to stop and take a deep breath. There was no possible way I could have walked home. I called for a ride to take me to my doctor. When I arrived, the staff drew some blood from my arm and set me up in an examining room. The doctor came in and checked me all over, including my cervix area, and left the room. I still felt terrible. A few minutes went by before he returned to the room, shook my hand, and said, "Congratulations!"

"To what?" I responded.

He said, "You are four months pregnant. Your due date is May 9th."

I went crazy in the head. For one thing, I'm thinking, no way am I pregnant, and another because that was my graduation date. He helped me off the table. I was in shock. He led me to another room where a lady *would show me the baby and I can possibly know what the sex was that day.* With no hesitation, the lady put the cold jelly on my stomach. She rubbed my belly and she said, "Well this baby didn't keep us guessing. He has his legs wide open. Congratulations on your baby boy."

All I could think about was, *what I'm going to do with another baby?* My mind was flipping in circles. I cried and cried. I was lost. Everything started to crumble inside of me. There was no way I could work and go to school without support. I prayed, crying out to God. I had to make a very hard decision to stop going to school so I could support my family. This wasn't easy for me at all. It had always been my heart's desire to finish school. I was just four months away from walking across the stage. Now my dreams were being put on hold again because I chose to disobey God; pleasing my needs that had caused me a lifetime of pain. This was my third time withdrawing from school. Why didn't I take heed when God was speaking to me trying to warn me? *Now look at me on baby #2, and out of wedlock?* How could I make my life better when I constantly kept going backwards? But there was no turning back. It was time to focus on my kids.

When I went to school to withdraw, the woman asked why I was withdrawing again, since I was so close to graduating. I explained to her that I was with child and didn't have a support system to help. She encouraged me to come back the following fall semester to finish and never give up. Those words warmed my heart. But I was still hurting because I had to choose between school and work - a decision that was so critical, it caused more pain that added to the earlier pain in my life.

I'm walking and I get on the street that takes me all the way to my job. I stood there on the sidewalk breaking down in tears, saying to myself, *my life has fallen apart if I only would have listened. I'm tired of not having help, I'm tired doing everything on my own.* I quickly had to get myself together. I had a life inside of me. I didn't want to stress or cause myself to be sick as if I wasn't already going through enough. I finally calmed myself enough to start back walking so I could get to work. I didn't want to go. I hated my job, but I knew I had bills to pay so I just said a prayer before entering. I couldn't stand all the fakeness that came along with my job. As I clocked in, I explain to my manager that I had to stop going to school because I found out I was four months pregnant. She said she knew I was pregnant.

I asked, "How did you know?"

"From my drug screening."

I was like wow and you didn't say anything.

"She said, "I couldn't. It's against corporate policy."

But overall, she gave me more hours and insisted that I worked the morning shift throughout the week and nights on weekends. I was fine with that. My mind began to race because I really didn't know how I was going to tell Jaden. You would think I wouldn't know who my child's father was because of how whorish I had been. But the smartest thing I could have done was to keep a diary with the date, day, and time with every man I had sex with because I was indeed wild.

The day was exhausting. I started to feel sick and light headed so the manager let me off work early. When I made it home, I took a shower, relaxed, and got on Facebook. It was my intentions to write Jaden in his inbox; to tell him I was pregnant. But I glanced through my friend request, and to my surprise, I had received a request from Devon, a guy I dated seven years ago. I accepted. Afterwards, I wrote Jaden,

I went to the doctor today because I wasn't feeling well. My doctor came in the room telling me congratulations, you are four months pregnant. And oh yeah, I'm having a boy. Due date May 9.

Jaden was excited and happy, so he said. But I couldn't tell because he asked me for a blood test, which was perfectly fine with me. I said sure you can have one because I knew it was his child. I'm thinking to myself now how foolish can I be to be pregnant with another woman's man's baby again? I was involved, tangled up, in this mess and things were about to become very stormy. Jaden and I stopped writing and Devon wrote me saying, "Hey!" Asking how I was doing. He gave me his number to call him, and he wanted to know if we could get back together. I was going through so much crazy stuff, I didn't have time for the whole relationship thing again so insisted that we be friends until otherwise.

I crawled out of bed because I felt myself falling into depression; to only set in the corner. It was extremely dark in my apartment. The depression covered in on my mind silently killing my mental state. Although I knew this wasn't good for my baby, I wept and wept. It was a form of release to keep me calm, but I noticed every time I cried my baby would be extremely still. He was always humbled when I would go into my dark place. I couldn't understand what was going on with me, but I still prayed to God because I couldn't get over the fact that I was having another baby.

I went back to bed because I needed my rest for work the next day. Tossing and turning all night, I didn't get as much sleep as I thought I would. My back was hurting so I sat up and ending up falling asleep sitting up. I jumped because I felt myself falling over as the bright sun hit my face and my eyes opened. It was time for me to get ready for work. *I'm moving slow because of a lack of sleep and just to think I have to walk makes me dread going to work, period.*

I had gotten so big. All I wanted to do was to eat and sleep. But I knew, with what needed to be done, and what I was going through, I couldn't afford to do that. As I walked to work, tears flowed, sticking to my face from the cool breeze. I was so over everything, and the people I thought were for me, had clearly left me when everything turned out for the worse. I stopped walking. I was tired and I was hurting everywhere. I was almost at work, so I kept moving forward, dragging myself. This job was taking all my energy during my pregnancy. I was always stressed and always had an attitude about something. As soon as I walked through the doors, one of my co-workers said, "That can't be Skyye walking to work."

I didn't say anything, but just smiled and clocked in. I started to work, and it didn't take me long to catch on. I knew my routine before opening time. I loved to do everything except make biscuits. OMG! That was like the hardest thing to do, plus I'm left handed, which made matters worse. The process was so difficult. I started to feel pain in the lower part of my stomach and I just stood there, breathing slowly, until the pain went away.

Customers started to flow in fast, so I had to be on my p's and q's, moving to stay ahead and be on it. I felt myself getting so sick but I still worked, although I knew I needed to slow it down. I was working too hard, plus I didn't get the proper rest that I needed the night before. When everything finally eased up, I hurried to the rest room. Sitting on the floor of the bathroom, I broke down. For sure, I was at my breaking point. Gone! I wasn't sure if I was lost or found. I was tired but all in all I never gave up. I kept fighting because I knew soon, God was going to work everything out for my good.

Within a few minutes, I regained my composure and returned to work, only to see the line had backed up. I'm saying to myself *where did all these people come from.* I still wasn't feeling my best. I just wanted to clock out and walk out. While making my way to the front, I heard someone calling my name. I leaned over the counter and it was Joel. He was my *on-and-off* since high school days. I was excited to see him because I'd always been crazy about him. He gave me his number telling me to call him when I got off work. I supposed he only came in when he saw me because he didn't even order any food. As he was walking out the door, he turned around with a smile saying, "I'll be looking forward to your phone call."

I wondered why people from my past had started to show back up in my life; all of a sudden. But I didn't ponder too long. I was anxious to get home and call Joel. He always had a laugh for me. We used to sit on the phone for hours laughing and helping one another cope through life.

The time finally came for me to clock out. I was starving. Not literally, but I was hungry. Could you blame me? I was pregnant and my craving was kicking in for those spicy tenders with mash potatoes. I had to have it before I went home. Normally, I would eat at home but that day, I sat right there and ate while I waited for my ride. I started feeling sick and I couldn't finish my food. I put my head down on the table and I must admit, my mind drifted to a faraway land. I wasn't on earth. I had so much on my mind, but I figured since I didn't have to work the next day, I needed to give God some of my time. I decided to call my aunt so she could pick me up later that week and I could attend Church with them.

Soon after ending the conversation with my aunt, my ride was outside. The minute I got in the car, I texted Joel instead of calling him. We texted back and forth until I made it home. I really had to be enjoying him because when I fell asleep, I slept good. My mind was at ease with much peace. I felt a sense of comfort come over my body. It had been a very, very long time since I felt that way. Was it temporary? I was not sure but I would ride with the feeling until it faded away.

I lie there trying to get into a comfortable position, switching sides over and over, and interrupted my good sleep. I couldn't go back so I got up and cooked me a full course meal at 3:00 in the morning. While the food cooked, I wrote a list to myself as to what all was coming soon. I listed eight goals that I needed to accomplish. I prayed over the piece of paper and stuck in my bible. I believed so I knew I was going to receive.

Church was starting in a few hours, and I looked in my closet, realizing all my clothes had gotten too little so it was tights and a sweater for me. Still, I was hurting so badly, my heart to be exact, I needed a touch from God. I knew he was the only one who could heal me. I was living in brokenness. I was lonely, I was afraid, I was fearful, I was ashamed, I was tired, and I was confused. My life didn't make a bit of sense and I just didn't know what to do. I believed if someone touched me, I would fall into a million pieces on the floor from all the chaos going on inside me.

My thoughts took a shift when I received a message from Joel. *Good morning beautiful. Have a good day.* What a way to start my morning? Right after, my aunt called to tell me she was pulling up to my door in about five minutes and be looking out. I was still on the couch texting Joel, and by reading his messages, I was thinking, *Joel wants to get serious with me.* Foolishly, I said to myself, "Now two people wanted a relationship with me. I should be with both of them. I didn't mind."

My aunt was outside blowing the horn and fortunately that blew and threw my thoughts off. As I walked down the stairs, my body started to pain. "Not today devil. I'm going to Church. I need to be refreshed and much prayer."

In my heart, I was willing to change. I was fed up with the way I was living. I was tired of hurting. I needed something new. All I could feel once I entered the Church was God's presence. The atmosphere was so clear, the Spirit of the Lord was most certainly there. As service and praises went up, I worshiped, giving God all the thanks for just being Him. During altar call, the request came if anyone needed prayer, a re-visit with God, or a healing. As the tears flowed, all that was requested was just for me. Something I had been longing for. As prayer flowed, I burst out with every scream that could come out. I let every ounce of hurt out of me, leaving it on the altar. God touched me right where I stood. He did something so wonderful to my spirit, I couldn't explain it if I wanted too. I got chills just thinking about how he renewed my mind, body, and soul. This was only the beginning. After receiving this prayer, I knew God had some great things in store for me. It was time for me to rededicate my life back to Christ. I wanted to be in Church more. After all, I had been a backslider for more than two years. It was time for me to get back under the submission to God's will.

Joel called me asking if he could come over later. I said "Sure why not? I would love to see you." It had been a minute since we chilled or just hung out. I'm assuming he was already outside. Within four or five minutes, he knocked on the door. I opened it, smiling, and he embraced me with a big hug.

He asked, "Are you hungry?"

"I'm always ready to eat, Joel." We both laughed.

"Okay, let me prep the food. You just sit down and relax." He continued talking. "You know, Skyye, I want to take care of you. I want to give this relationship thing a try only if you agree. I don't want to pressure you into anything. I mean, we have known each other for years and something always came in the way. I just know this is fate because we met again."

I was flattered, in awe. It all felt good but as my mind overthought like normal, *Will I be making the right decision? Am I what he needs? Will he be as loyal as he's talking?* I did myself the honor of shaking those thoughts off and told him yes, this relationship maybe everything I need and more.

I really didn't think it was a good idea to do this because I was in a place where I had found God again and had opened my heart up to him totally. But if I could fight the temptation to fornicate, I could make it. I had been doing good so far. I really wanted to see where this relationship would go. I was nervous but sort of /kind of happy. I felt as if I was in a new space in life. My brain was exhausted. I had to work the next day and I couldn't sleep. Tears began to flow, and thoughts of my grandma fell on my heart so heavy. I sat up doing what I loved to do - writing poetry. That freed my mind and took me to a calm place of relaxation. I knew it would shake the feeling of thinking about my grandma. I had five hours until I had to be at work, so I closed my eyes to get some rest, and I began to dream:

"I was headed to minister. I had an assignment from God and Joel stopped me telling me to never leave him; he needs me. I tell him I will be back. Somehow, he locked me in a room with people coming towards me; destroying me. I was cut in my side five times. The people were all my exes; lined up attacking me on every end. I started running, forgetting all about my assignment for God. It was two lanes, left and right, and God said, "It's your choice. I'm warning you! It's either Heaven or Hell." Then He disappeared"

I woke up terrified because harm was coming my way and I think God was trying to get me prepared. I didn't completely understand the dream. Shaking my head, I went on dragging around the house, calling people, trying to find a ride to work. Sad to say, I had to walk. All I'm thinking in my head, *I'm about to quit I'm sick of this.* I couldn't call Joel because he was at work himself. As I walked, I pondered on the dream but at the same time, I ignored it. I wanted to be with Joel. I was sure I could benefit some way from this relationship. At least that's what I was thinking. I started hurting so bad in the bottom of my stomach. I had to stop and sit down on the side of the curb to breathe. Mind you, it was as cold as ever. I couldn't do anything but cry, *where is everyone when I need them?* God and prayer were the only things I could depend on.

I forced myself up because I knew I had to be at work. I made it on time. I clocked in and started on the biscuits before we opened, and the same pain came the way I experienced walking to work. I wasn't sure if I was in labor or having Braxton Hicks contractions. I went to the restroom and found that the leaking was blood and mucus mixed together. I told my manager I needed to go plus I hadn't felt Baby Boy move for a whole day. I was freaking out. I really felt like no one cared about me. They only cared about me getting the job done because the manager was mad when I had to leave. It was hard enough already dealing with stuff off my job plus the job was working me like a slave. As bad as I wanted to tell her *I quit,* I couldn't. After all, I had to support my kids. I just clocked out and waited for someone to take me to the emergency room.

I checked in at the ER and was called at once. The nurse said my blood pressure was through the roof and I was indeed stressed. She recommended that I go ahead and go to the second floor to be watched because they didn't feel the baby moving at all either. When I walked up to the desk, this pretty white lady asked who sent me because she didn't see my name on the screen. I told her the issue and she hurried from behind the desk and had me in a room giving me instructions on what to do. I had a button in my hand that I needed to push every time the baby moved. We talked and in a short period of time, we had a whole conversation about a lot of things. She left out and I closed my eyes calling on Jesus. Suddenly Baby Boy kicked, and he kicked. It's something about that name that has so much power in it. I had to keep calling on him. She came in to rub my stomach saying Baby Boy you're having a field day in there. We both laughed. She insisted that I go home to rest but mainly stay off my feet. If only she knew the struggle was indeed real for me. A single parent of two who had to drop out of college to provide for my family; working hard trying to make ends meet all while trying to keep it all together from life's crisis itself. I glanced at her name tag to remember her name. She had taken really good care of me and I wanted to show my appreciation the next time I saw her. I left feeling so much better. Thanks to God and her assistance.

I didn't return to work. I went straight home and rested, wanting to nap, but I thought about the information I needed so Zion could go to daycare. After pulling all the paperwork together, I walked to the daycare and turned it in. Zion was accepted and qualified for the childcare assistance program so that meant she could start the next day. I was excited about that. I had a few people watching after her and they were charging me. That was another financial burden on me. The daycare was convenient for me since we lived right down the street. I didn't have a problem with walking her each day because I too had to walk to work anyway. It was a struggle but we maintained it with God's help. My phone rang and it was Joel checking on me. I texted him earlier to inform him that I was at the ER. He rushed over to see me. I knew then he cared about me. It was sweet. Not only that, he wanted to be involved with anything that took place with me. So I saw that he was serious about what we had said. God brought that dream back to mind. I ignored it. I asked Joel did he want to spend the night with me. He said yeah since we both had to be at work at 4 p.m. plus he didn't want me walking. He showed concern about my health as I carried Baby Boy.

We stayed up talking, laughing, dancing, singing trying to find baby names and I did come up with a name - Jabari Jareed. Wasn't sure about the last name yet though but overall we were just enjoying each other's company. My pregnant self was hungry around my normal time at three in the morning. He took me out to eat at Huddle House and we sat there eating discussing life issues and what we needed to do to overcome every obstacle we faced. Our conversations were always deep. Now full and sleepy, I couldn't move. Joel had to help me up. We left to go back to the house; he opened the door and helped me get in the car. A song came on the radio and he started singing to me, reaching over to kiss me on the jaw. He was always sweet to me. One thing I did know, he kept a smile on my face. We made it in the house and he kissed me again but this time on the lips. He whispered how much he loved me. I didn't say it back, I was still smiling. He rubbed me on my legs.

I said, "Are you sure this is what you want to do?"

"I need you Skyye."

I went into deep thought. My flesh told me to go on and have sex with him, while my spirit, alarming loud, said No! I tried to fight that temptation as hard as I could. I gave in; we end of having sex. The moment we finished, I felt God's conviction all over me. I couldn't do anything but cry. I knew what I did was wrong, now I must face the consequences for what took place. I know God is about to punish me in the worse ways. I fell short of his glory and moved on my own. God was dealing with me so hard I couldn't even sleep. I stayed up. Besides, it was pointless for me to go to sleep. It was nearly time for my doctor's appointment before heading to work.

I took a shower and put on my work clothes; waking Joel up with a kiss on his neck so he can get up to take me to check on Baby Boy. On our way to the doctor, he asked what I wanted to eat. I was craving for Popeye's spicy chicken. He said we would get something to eat there before dropping me off at work. I was excited; Joel went with me on my doctor visit. He was supportive; he even went to the back room with me to see the baby. We discovered that Baby Boy gained two pounds and five ounces. He was really growing. I was still in shock about bringing another life into this world so I just stared at the sonogram. I was so thrilled to meet this little happy baby who would always smile.

We picked up our food on the way to work. Sitting in the car, eating and talking, Joel goes to say he wanted to move in. I didn't think that would be a good idea. I assured him that we could only do that if we were married. "I mean, I have already messed up by having sex with you."

He said he understood and he didn't want to rush anything. Still, I did give him a key to my apartment, allowing him to go and come as he pleased. We kissed. I got out the car and the minute I got in the door at work, I began to hurt. I'm like, *Oh no, o-my-gosh, I have to be at work until two in the morning.* I didn't have time for this and all the extra that came with the job.

God spoke to me telling me I have made a mistake. I didn't take heed to the dream and I must suffer with the decision I made. Tears formed because I knew something was about to take place. I started back working to distract myself from crying. I was sneaking texting Joel and he wasn't responding. Wasn't supposed to have my phone but I called him and called him again. Still nothing and this was not like him. I couldn't wait to get off to give him a piece of my mind. Instead of getting off at two, I ended up getting off at midnight because I was hurting very bad. I couldn't function. I felt myself being stressed and the last thing I was about to do was run up behind a man. I'm thinking to myself, *I messed up giving him this key. Man, why did I ignore my dream? Now I have to deal with this.*

I found a ride home. Not wasting anytime, as soon as I got home, I fell in the bed because sleep was all I needed at that point. I didn't sleep long as I expected. Woke up no call back nor had he shown up yet. I sent him a long stupid message with no kind words. He still didn't reply so I called one more time. The phone picked up. I'm saying hello but I don't hear anyone. I'm assuming his phone is in his pocket so being me, I held the phone, put it on mute as I recorded the phone conversation. He was supposed to have been at work. He's at another woman's house. The conversation was everything I needed to hear. My heart cracked into pieces to hear him tell her the same things he told me. I felt so worthless and useless. I felt like a fool because I thought we had something real.

I texted him again as I sit there crying my heart out, saying B***H bring my key it's over, I'm done! He started calling and calling. My attitude was through the roof. He ended up showing up, coming up with lies while I never mentioned I heard the conversation. I let him tell all his lies. I smiled thinking it's my turn now. Staring at him, I pull my phone out, pressing the recorded phone conversation, putting it on speaker. His mouth wide open, trying to apologize, saying how he can make it up.

I said, "It's over."

"Skyye, let me make love to you."

He started kissing on me. I pushed him away. He grabbed me. I said "NO! I don't want sex. Go and never come back."

So, he went down on me; the best *Goodbye* present I could have received. And when he finished, I put him out, blocked him, and stayed away from him with much distance. Why didn't I listen to God? He tried to warn me this would happen. I prayed to God because there was no other way I could heal from the pain. I was hurting. Those sweet nothings and pillow talks had me swimming in the head. I was distracted and confused much. I needed God. I prayed, I cried, I prayed some more while the tearing never stopped flowing. I cried myself to sleep.

I woke up to a knock on the door. It was Zion coming home. She runs up to me and kisses my stomach first, then gives me a kiss on my lips. I needed that. We lay down on the couch watching cartoons and eating our favorite white cheddar popcorn. As she lay there with her face on my stomach, she pointed to it saying, "That's my baby, Ma. He mines." Then she smiled at me. She just doesn't know how that warmed my heart. That comfort made my world go around.

We got up to get ready for the next day. I had to go to work and she had to attend her first day at daycare. Shortly after that, we had our baths and got in bed, tears started to fall from my eyes. I didn't want her to see me cry but she ended up doing so. She said, "Ma, it's going to be okay."

I broke down as she lay next to me holding me tight until she fell asleep. My heart was so damaged; I slid from under her to go in the living room because my depression had set in on me. I scooped down, falling on my knees, bending over rocking backwards and forward, as the darkness began to suffocate me. My mind was full of turmoil. I was broken and just wanted to be whole. I cried more tears and I ended up falling to sleep in the corner. I heard Zion's footsteps as she sat on my leg, then lying down on my stomach. I opened my eyes and I thought it was so sweet how she tried to help me up. I started to get her ready. During that process, I went to the bathroom. I peed and as I wiped myself, I saw nothing but blood. My heartbeats grew faster. I was scared and shaking. I felt like I was going crazy in the head. I called my cousin and I told him what happened. He got to my house quickly, dropped Zion off at the daycare, and got me to the clinic as fast as he could.

At the clinic, the doctor said what was happening to me wasn't normal. He checked to find out that I was 8 1/2 centimeters from having my baby. He could have been born at any minute and I had no idea I was in labor. He pulled me off the table telling me we had to get this baby out of me, and QUICK! I'm nervous, I'm shaking and steady trying to call someone, anyone. Finally, I got hold of my aunt informing her that Jabari was on his way. My doctor took my phone. He saw how distracted and frustrated I was. He swerved his truck around to the door, picked me up, and put me in to drive me across to the ER. He saw the fear in my face. The nurses came with a wheel chair. I mean everyone was moving like robots. I was on the second floor before I knew it. The pains started to come, the tears rolled uncontrollably. I'm real deal scared for my life because I can die, my son can die, or it could be us both. My doctor assured me that we were going to be okay. "Breathe, Skyye, and do what the nurses ask of you. They are here to help prep you for surgery."

I'm crying harder now because I'm like, *No, I have to have another C- Section.* This time it was urgent. They hooked me up to everything. I had never seen nurses move so fast.

My son coming at 29 weeks was too early, labeling it as a premature stage. It was a real emergency. They double-checked twice to make sure everything was correct. After doing so, they rolled me down to have surgery. A man was standing next to me, asking me questions as he put the medicine in my IV to make me fall asleep. My doctor asked, "Do you feel this?"

I screamed as I felt the razor go across my stomach. I felt when he cut me open. He injected more medicine in my IV and he repeated the question. By then, I was numb and loopy. I was hallucinating, fighting, pulling my mask off three times. One nurse grabbed my hand rubbing while the other nurse rubbed my head. I calmed down, speaking in my mind, *Lord, let your will be done.*

I was out of it. My head swung over to the side. I went into a deep sleep shortly. I woke up throwing up everywhere. The pain was unbearable. Drowsy, I asked about my son repeatedly as they rolled me to the recovery room. I had been cut in the same spot from the first C-Section, but I didn't mind risking my life so my son could be here. It just seemed so surreal to repeat the cycle again. He made his grand entrance at 9:00 A.M. weighing 2 pounds and 8 ounces. I was excited but still no Jabari. I was getting furious because he was nowhere to be found. My heart burned so bad not seeing my son. All I wanted to do was hold him, kiss him, and tell him how proud I was to be his mom.

Unfortunately, they had called the nurses from Greenville, Mississippi Neonatal Intensive Care Unit (NICU) to transport Jabari because he needed special care. I was emotional, I'm weeping because I didn't see him, I'm suffering, my depression is silently killing me, suicidal thoughts roaming, I was lost on every end. As I lie there trying to get some rest, my phone rang. The lady from the apartments that I had applied for way back when I first came back from Georgia a year ago called. She said she had an opening available for a 2-bedroom apartment if I was still interested. "Look at God," was all I could say. I'm in awe. I told her YES! And explaining to her that I was in recovery from just having a baby two days ago. She insisted that the apartment was mine and to get well. She said she would have it ready for me by the end of the month. He doesn't show up when you want Him to, but He is always on time. I couldn't stop smiling after going through all that. My second MIRACLE HAD BEEN DELIVERED :) I love God and I have never been ashamed to praise Him. I had to give Him thanks. I knew it was nobody but Him.

I was hurting but my praise had to go up not only for that apartment but for my son's healing as well. I got a knock on the door and it was the pretty white lady from the desk with the initials C.J. She came to talk to me about breastfeeding; giving me the odds and ends and how it was very important for my son's life. I went for it; started that same night. She told me she would be with him for the rest of the week and if I needed her to call. She even gave me her personal number and after she showed me how to use the pump, she left the room.

I called Jaden to tell him I had Jabari and that he was born earlier than what we thought. He came to see me and to sign the birth certificate. He seen a picture of him and was like, "Wow, he looks like my oldest son. Yeah he is most definitely mines."

I gave him the number so he could call whenever he got ready. He had to get back to work while I'm trying to push myself up out the bed because I'm ready to go home. This hospital bed was uncomfortable, and I was having separation anxiety. It was killing me. I began to get up to walk and fell back. The staples were painful. I asked God for much strength and tried it again. Finally, I was up and walking every step. It hurt but I had to make progress. As I walked, my thoughts flowed. I was broken in every area of my life. I couldn't seem to find a place of healing. I was still empty inside while God was already in the present waiting to give me what I longed for. I was too stubborn to open my heart giving Him all I had because I thought I had it all figured out. As I walk towards the room, I call to check on my son. They said he was doing okay; sleeping. That gave me relief. My doctor came in, checked my stomach, and encouraged me to keep walking so I could go home.

Devon called me and started ministering to me. If only he knew how badly I needed that word from God. He also prayed with me and for me so that really helped me get through the days I had left in the hospital. I hung up from him as my medicine was kicking in. I needed my rest. I wasn't feeling my best at all. I was still loopy, falling in and out of depression. I cried just about every day. Often times, I asked myself why am I here? My life was a living hell. I just didn't see a purpose in all the pain. I started to think about my son, so I called to check on him again. They said he was doing fine and encouraged me to keep pumping because he was enjoying mommy's milk. I smiled hanging up the phone. My nurse came in to check on me and to tell me that my doctor was letting me go home the next day, the best news I had heard so far. Besides, I was ready to get to my kids. I missed them both like crazy and I just didn't feel right without them. My life was sucked dry because my kids were the only real Joy and Hope I had when I started to feel empty inside. I couldn't risk living life without them; it would be pointless. I pondered about life and the decisions I had to make to stay on the right path with God. Half of the time, I didn't know which way to go. Brokenness was the result of my self-will leaving God, no room to heal, and because I always stayed true to myself, I was never afraid of being who I was. I was able to deal with the issues accordingly.

FINALLY! I was being discharged, getting ready to leave the hospital as they check my stomach and prep to get the IV out my hand. I closed my eyes tight as the nurse removed the IV. I heard God speak loud and clear, "It's purpose in your pain." I opened my eyes and the needle wasn't there anymore. Thank you, Jesus. I called my cousin to come get me so I could get home. Shortly after conversing with him, I called the lady who had contacted me from the new apartment, letting her know I was out of the hospital. She told me to bring a money order for my deposit and since

I was moving in at the end of the month, she would kindly reduce my rent to a certain amount. Being that I had to be in the house for six weeks, I let my cousin take care of everything while I tried to get some rest. The moment I got relaxed, a knock on the door. I'm like, "Shoot." Pushing up, and moving at a steady pace, opening the door, it's the pretty white lady from the desk, CJ, coming by with breastfeeding items to continue with the process.

I began to talk with her with tears in my eyes and discouragement in my voice, "CJ, I have no support and I don't have the slightest idea how I will get to and from Greenville to supply my son with his milk."

She gladly said the days that she worked she would come by. And because she knew I was in healing process, she smiled telling me she would love on him sending videos and pictures. I knew then she was my angel on earth sent from God. My Third Miracle Delivered.

The Tylenol 3s were kicking in hard. I was falling asleep texting, but the message never made it. My phone rang extremely loud. I jumped. It was the hospital calling. I missed the call, so I called back. They said that Jabari had stopped breathing twice. They had to put him on a ventilator to help him breathe due to his under-developed lungs. I think my heart stopped for two seconds, and tears rolled fast as the nurse comforted me on the phone. She explained how brave and strong my child was, and that he was fighting to live. She said he fought and he's back breathing. Just not being there had me crushed inside. I got on my computer and played Pandora Gospel station and William McDowell's "Withhold Nothing" came on. I burst into crying, pleading, and talking to God. I gave it all to Him. No more half-stepping and no more doing things my way. Oh, how that song ministered to my soul. I cried, feeling my heart heal. My mind became clearer, my spirit uplifted; feeling so refreshed when all those burdens were rising off me.

I had to praise God for my son. Praying and drawing closer to Him, I couldn't see it any other way. Nothing else was working. God got my attention and I'm glad he did. It was time to move forward and to new beginnings. I started packing although I had at least two weeks to move from old to new. I had my keys already. I was amazed how God worked that thing out so fast. God made a way for my kids and myself when everyone counted me out, talked about me, didn't help. He made an example out of my life to show them he was still there, despite of anything that I was facing. I was able to depend on Him and not people. Are you healed yet? Are chains being broken? The journey continues. Come on ride it out with me. We're ALMOST THERE!

Crowned Butterfly

I have a tattoo of a "Colorful Butterfly" that's placed on my upper right shoulder and it symbolizes the freedom that's in me. Life at this point is less stressful, carefree, and I'm happy.

As I moved into my new apartment, I felt like a butterfly with beautiful wings. Life seemed as wonderful as I looked to the future and the newness that was taking over. My life blossomed into purity, love, joy and much happiness. To my surprise, it didn't take us 24 hours to move so I was able to not only unpacked but also sort out our belongings to my liking. I had to keep things in order. It wouldn't be me if I didn't organize. I was excited, on a new path, a new start, a new journey, a new and improved walk with God. As I listened to my worship music, God spoke to me saying, *Expect all great things to come to pass. You have put old things to rest and made the ultimate sacrifice to live for me as a new creature in Christ. Look for your blessings to flourish this year.*

126

The first thing I thought about was my expectancy list. I smiled, thanking God and just praising Him for what he had done and was about to do. I continued sorting and organizing, would have finished but tiredness took over, and I reclined on the couch. I called to check on my kids. While Zion was with her other family, Jabari was still in the hospital. I missed them both and was so anxious for them to see the new apartment that God has blessed us with. The day had been long and exhausting, and I prayed and prayed until I drifted off to sleep. Again, I dreamed:

I found myself in this empty dark room where there was no feature. As I entered the room, a sense of curiosity, fear, and wonderment stirred within me. I randomly touched walls and these feelings went all through my body. Some brought joy, sweet memories, sense of shame, and regrets. It was so intense, I felt a mix of emotions cloud my heart and mind. It was clear that I was overwhelmed by the sheer life I had lived; a rough life. When I glanced at the wall again, I saw the lustful desires for men, the distasteful music, the depression, the brokenness that took over my life, the defeat and helpless ways I faced. The tears came; I wept and sobbed so deeply that it shook through me as my stomach felt the pain. I cried out of shame. I saw nothing but my past life. I pushed the tears away as I saw Jesus. He walked over and put His arm around me. He didn't say a word, He just cried with me. He told me to look at the wall again. I saw His blood stains covering my sins, my guilt, and my shame. As His light showered the wall in that dark room, it was alive with his blood. He smiled at me and said, "IT IS FINISHED."

My phone rang and I jumped. It was the General Manager from my job asking me if I was returning to work after my maternity leave was up. I said yes. She put me back in the system so when I returned to work, the paperwork would already be finished, and I could start back without delay. Although I didn't want to go back to that job, I needed the money. I was in awe and my mind was just blown from the dream I had. I saw myself going through the moment of transitioning. I didn't need revelation from God. The full effect of my life was being played out before my eyes. The pretty lady from the desk, CJ, came by to see if I wanted a ride to the hospital with her. That way I would be able to see my baby. I got my bag ready and headed out the door, but I realized I wasn't ready to spend the night with him yet. I called my cousin to let him know that I would need a ride back home. While CJ and I rode together in the car, there was pure silence the whole ride. I was very uncomfortable. We said a few casual words, finally, not much. I was too busy observing. That's how I learn a person. I knew it would take some time and eventually I would get use to her, but I thought, for now I'll just enjoy the ride. We made it to the hospital and the time had come for me to see my son. I was elated.

Before entering the room, I whispered a little prayer asking God to give me the strength to hold up. I took a deep breath and walked slowly to the incubator. I broke down. Tears flowed heavily as I saw him covered with IVs and tubes, all patched on him from head to toe. Seeing how small he was made me cry the loudest and draw closer to God. There was no way I could get through this alone. I had to have the prayers from my Church family and Jesus as well because I knew I couldn't fight this battle alone. My son needed me, and I finally pulled myself together. I leaned over the glass that separated me from my joy. He held my pinky finger as I placed my hand in the window, gripping tightly, and holding on not wanting to let go. This was one of my biggest fears, that he wouldn't know me. But as he continued to hold, I felt comfortable and warm. The Spirit of God was on me heavy. He spoke to me: *No more giving me half of you. You have to give me your whole life. You must do so to receive your son's life.*

I was just getting back in tune with God so I understood I couldn't compromise or gamble with this. I had a purpose that needed to be fulfilled through God's will and the only way to do it was to give myself away so He could use me.

Soon it was time for my postpartum checkup. I went to the doctor and everything was great and normal. More importantly, it was a clean slate for me to start practicing celibacy. I was at a point in my life where I was ready to be married and have a family. My heart's biggest desire. But for that to happen, I had to be submissive to God, following his ways and not mine. Any sacrifices I had to face, I was willing to take the offer including losing everyone because I wanted to live for Jesus only.

I took the paperwork from my doctor to my job saying I could start back to work the next day. I was so happy everything was falling in place and looking up for me. I came home. God told me to write five poems a day, and every time I write, my son would heal. I said, "Okay, Lord."

The minute I stepped in the door at my home, I started writing; writing none stop. I wrote so much, I had fallen asleep. But here's the catch. I'm sure it's going to blow your mind because I'm still in awe of what I thought was sleep, wasn't sleep. Nor was it a dream. It was a quick visit from God. Here it goes:

I went lifeless for three minutes. I felt my soul rise out of my body. Not only that, I saw myself lying on the couch holding the paper and pen as if I were sleeping. I had transitioned into another phase of life. I heard water flashing against my body as I begin to sink. I started floating and as I'm floating, I hear an annoying hospital beep, crazy loud noise that constantly alarmed. The minute I hit the gate the beep stopped. I look up and the gates began to open. I never saw anything so beautiful, and then I saw God. He looked at me, smiled, and said welcome back my daughter. You belonged here all along. You don't have to be afraid. As long as you walk with Me daily, you can live without being fearful to live for Christ.

I was dead for those minutes. I gasped for air; waking up with a call in my spirit that only wanted to praise God and lift up His name. I just couldn't stop worshipping Him. Soon my phone goes off and it was one of the nurses from NICU telling me that Jabari IVs and tubes had been removed. He was making progress, gaining weight and would be coming home in the next two weeks if he kept up the good work. My God, my son was partaking in his healing just as God spoke to me. There was no way I could ever doubt God again after He showed His unchanging hands in my son's life. My mind was blown at how God moved within seconds. I was just overwhelmed of how awesome God is. It's a good feeling; such a feeling that I couldn't describe.

Devon sent me a text asking if he could see me. I told him maybe another time since I had to work the next day. He switched the conversation saying he couldn't stop thinking about me and he didn't want to just be with me, he wants to marry me. I told him let's see what God has to say because after what went down with Joel, I couldn't risk another heartache. I didn't have the time or energy to continuously repeat the same cycles. I ended up falling to sleep texting him. When I opened my eyes, I gave my day to God in prayer and reading the bible before getting prepared for work. After seeking God, I got dressed and headed out the door. I walked to work because I was over calling around trying to get a ride. Before I made it out of my apartment complex there was a woman offering me a ride. I had to give God thanks right then and there and give this woman thanks for her act of kindness. I knew it was God. He always sends a stranger to bless you in a mighty way big or small. Anything God does for me is a big deal, and I am forever grateful.

The moment I stepped out the car walking into my job my coworkers' spirits start riding me. I was so burdened down and being that I didn't live the lifestyle I once lived, a major change took place within me. Instead of the demons being with me, they were now against me. I'm whispering under my breath THE BLOOD OF JESUS as much as I could, and the Spirit of God overtook my body. I was free, the devil had to flee. *I can do all things through Christ that strengthens me* is the scripture that helped me make it through the day. I said it five times before working. I clocked in, started doing what I supposed to do but I was not feeling it. I felt like an outcast because now I must guard my heart, mind, spirit, and soul with my whole life. It was vital that I stayed to myself while everyone else said I was acting funny. It was never the case. It was God setting me aside from the world to be more like Him and less of myself.

While at work, I received a phone call from the hospital. Jabari had reached his weight goal and he would be coming home within a week or two. The time had come for me to let my job go and focus on Jabari's health. I had been advised that my son would need my care 24/7 and I had to be watchful and attentive to his needs. Yes, I trusted God, but I still hadn't yet got over my worrying. I tried to figure out how my bills would be paid without any income. I didn't think on it too much because I would fall into a depression. Also, before my son was discharged from NICU, I wanted to spend nights with him to get used to him. Each day CJ would have to work, she didn't mind at all picking me up to go with her. I didn't care how tired I was, I needed to be active in my son's life. Truth be told, I got tired of calling down there every two seconds. I wanted to be in his presence.

Riding with CJ became easier. We started to talk more, laugh more, share stories more and our main topic was always Jabari. We shared him together so now he was OUR son. I couldn't repay her if I wanted to, so I always showered her with gifts and expressed my love to her daily. She probably got tired of me, but I had to let her know how I truly felt. It was all from the heart. Sometimes Devon even went with me on the long hours of sitting and waiting to see Jabari. He made sure I had peace of mind; he would sit and read the bible with me, pray with me, and more. Those two, CJ and Devon, really stuck by my side with my son, and I couldn't thank them enough

When I finally got to see Jabari and I instantly smiled because the tubes, everything had been taken off of him. Like God promised me. I got to hold him and love on him. Tears flowed from my eyes as he clung to me, placing his hand in my shirt. Not wanting to let go or put him down, my heart was so happy. After my time of loving on him, I left the room as he lies there getting a restful sleep. I needed my rest too for work the next day. I was exhausted but anything for my son. I couldn't risk being away from him another second.

As I walk this life as a new Christian, I have come to the realization that I'm nothing without God, although I made (and still making) my mistakes. I'm not perfect. He still showered me with much mercy and grace. In fact, He forgave me, restored me, and now He's building me to be the woman He needs me to be for Him. I weep because Jesus has come into my heart. HE SAVED ME. I knew I wasn't right without God, but after facing so much on this journey, His Christ explained His undying love for me. I don't have to be burdened with sins from the past. I can continue to move on with a clean slate. All this is new for me, but I know God is going to see me through. He wouldn't dare let me face this alone. He did place people to help me cope. Even if it was for a lifetime or seasonal, I'm taking advantage of it and cherishing every moment.

I really didn't want to go to work. I hadn't had much sleep, plus I had to work from 9 AM until five that evening. Not mentioning I had to go straight to the hospital when I got off work to spend more time with my son. While at work, I explained to my boss that it was my last week there due to my son's condition. She asked questions as to how my bills would be paid. I simply said, "What I can't handle, God will make a way. I trust that he will provide a way."

She said, "If you leave, you will not be eligible for rehire."

I told her my son was way more important than this job and I walked off to work my shift. I had to be prepared because at that moment and time of my life, I didn't know what to expect, but I did know God was up to something. I finished my shift and headed straight to the hospital to see my son. When I arrived, it was time for his bath. Apparently, he didn't like baths, the way he was screaming. Afterwards, it was feeding time but this time with a bottle. They put him in my arms, and he was so fragile, I was scared I was going to drop him. I freaked out. The nurse said, "Mom, it's okay. If you want him to go home with you tomorrow, you have to make him suck this bottle."

I got so frustrated, I just couldn't do it. I tried to give him back to the nurse and she gave him right back. It wasn't a choice, it was mandated. I tried to give him the bottle, but he kept moving his mouth away. Can you believe I fought with my son all night and all he sucked was half of the bottle? I was so tired, I went to the room to get some sleep until it was his next feeding time. Well, I didn't get any sleep because Devon called me. I was on the phone all night. It was so much hitting me all at once. Tears begin to fall as I vented to him what was taking place. He called just in time of my need, boosting my spirit, encouraging me, and praying for me. I knew then I still loved him even from seven years ago because this is what he used to do back then. That night, we decided to give it a try again. Not because of what he had, but the way he always uplifted my spirit. I was convinced in my heart that he was the one. And I knew for sure he was a blessing from God to help me on this journey as a new creature in Christ and a single mother.

There was a knock on the door, and as I turned my head to wipe the tears away, the nurse insisted that I come down to feed Jabari. I got myself together took a deep breath, saying to myself, me and my son are going to get through this, let me try again. I understand why he's a fighter because I'm a fighter too, so we're going to fight this thing out together. When I went in to feed him, he was just kicking and playing. I picked him up and this time he didn't fight with me. He sucked the whole bottle. I was excited. He must have known that I didn't get any sleep. I couldn't even keep my eyes open as I sat there and watched them demonstrate his car seat, hearing, and eye test. I was amazed at how active and alert he was. He passed everything and he was as ready to go home as much as I wanted him there. I supposed.

We had a few more hours before leaving NICU. I gave CJ a big tight hug, just thanking her for being there. She didn't have to put up with me, but she did. She was truly an angel sent from God who had been guiding me through this tough journey; truly a blessing in our life. We sat around, ate, talked, and let the nurses love on Jabari, and as they did, we got the belongings in the car. I was emotional and overwhelmed. Yes, I was happy but fearful, as well because I would have to perform the duties of being a single mother for the second time with the help of others and not Jabari's father. I really didn't know how it was going to play out, but

I had faith that God was going to give me strength to pull through.

When we got in the car, CJ asked if I had any support. I told her I never had help, especially from family. She said, "Well, anything you need, call or text anytime."

I knew this was God. I couldn't do anything but cry silently inside without any form of tears. We made it home and getting settled, I didn't want to see anyone. I was exhausted mentally, and I knew the time would come when people would pop up out the woods, knocking on my door, to see my baby. People I hadn't heard from during my pregnancy and people I didn't even deal with, pretending like they were concerned or wanted to help. But I knew they only want to see who my son looks like and what he looks like. I can't tell you how many people came to my door. It was good I had a peephole. I could hear the knock, look, and go sit right back down. I was sitting staring at my son, rubbing his face while he slept, just thanking God for all that he was doing. My son fought to be here. He was a survivor, a strong brave child, and truly a supernatural miracle. God saw him through, and for that I knew God had a plan for my son's life.

I lie there with my son propped up on my chest until he was sound to sleep. I laid him down and God spoke to me, "It's time for you to go into another level in me. It's time to build up the strength to stand what you are about to face."

He instructed me to call on Jesus until I uttered in tongues, so I did what he said. Meditating, closing my eyes, and relaxing, I called on Jesus over and over again. I uttered in a language I had never experienced before. Was I scared? Heck yeah! I tried to stop but it forced itself out of my belly.

God told me not to fight it but keep going. The spirit was so high on me I felt like I was floating. I received the Holy Ghost right there in my home. God dealt with me right where I was. I felt the newness birth inside of me. God was in the midst. I felt so good as God did what he wanted to do with me. Now He had my attention fully and he knew this time I was serious about living for Him. I was focused. I was in tuned. I was ready. I was on my way.

I was still pondering on how my bills would get paid and the minute I kneeled to pray, I received a call from the job. My W-2 form was in for my taxes. God know your thoughts and He knows what you need and just because I was about to seek Him about a financial breakthrough, He opened a door for me. Before I filed my taxes, He challenged me to do some things. I always believed in paying my tithes in Church or out of Church. I made sure God got a portion of whatever I had. He spoke to me insisting that I plant a $1,070.00 seed and if I had told anyone, they would have said I was crazy. You are probably saying it too, but I knew what God could do and I know my faith level. He also told me to give all my clothes away - pants, shoes, and shirts. Not only that, makeup and jewelry, too. Now the hard part was waiting on God to unfold things. I didn't know when my blessing was going to come or how it would happen, but I trusted the process. I didn't waste any time filing my taxes because my bills were coming around again. I got my money back within two days. I knew it had to be God because it takes some weeks to get your money back. Before I did anything with my money, I took out what he wanted me to put in Church.

I paid my bills up for about four months and the rest I put up for a car. I felt really good about doing this.

As I called around to find a car, the Lord told me to call the pretty lady, CJ. I did and she said she was going to look around for me. I told her how much I had saved up she said she would do her best to help me get what I needed. When I hung up the phone, my doorbell rang. I looked through the peephole, but whoever it was had apparently left. There was something white hanging on the bar door. I opened the door widely to see an envelope addressed to me. It read, *For Skyye.* I opened it and above the seal it read, *This 1,000 dollars is for you.* I started shouting, dancing, speaking in tongues, just thanking God over and over again. I couldn't stop praising Him. My mind was blown. I went back in the house, closed my door, screaming, worshipping, crying, and just thanking God constantly in every way. I was so slayed in the spirit, I ended of falling to sleep. I dream again:

I was walking in a big parking lot. As I was looking around, I got lost and somehow, I walked upon a group of boys who were about to fight. One of the boys had some type of liquid and if it hit you, you would instantly burn, turning into fire, burned alive. But to prevent the liquid from getting on you, you had to jump on this wired fence to protect yourself. That's what I did. I was in the middle of a battle I knew nothing about. As the rage began to calm, I ended up walking into a big building with multiple stairs. There were two women standing upstairs hiding from the boys. They began to explain to stand in a certain spot because at some point, one of the boys was going to pour the liquid in the building to harm everyone. As I stood there, the liquid was falling all over the women. There was no fence to get on so I'm just running around, and God spared me.

When I woke up, my phone was ringing. It was Devon. He was going through some things, so we talked and prayed for a while. He asked if it was okay to spend a few nights at my place, as he needed to clear his mind. I said, "Sure. Well as long as you know you are sleeping on the couch."

He said he respected that and understood fully. He also mentioned that he wanted to help me around the house, and if the truth be told, I needed it. After we ended the conversation, I sat there thinking about my dream, asking God for a revelation because it bothered me, and my spirit was uneasy. I didn't feel right at all and I think something was about to happen. Right then and there God said, "The devil is going to try and attack you because you sowed that big seed; tempt you and distract you on every end. But if you keep your eyes on me you want lose focus."

And then it hit me. The more I do for God, the more the devil is going to ride me. I was not serving the devil anymore and doing worldly stuff. I'm sure God was about to remove the people that meant me no good, as well. Being that I'm saved, we were on two different paths, so I'm certain a disaster was about to happen. The dream was just too vivid not to believe so.

Devon finally made it to my house. We hugged, sat, and talked. I just couldn't keep the good news to myself. I had to tell the praise report of the Lord. I had to tell him how God came through so suddenly. He was amazed and in awe from all that God was doing for me and through me. He said, "Skyye, you have always been a big giver. God is always going to take care of you. You have such a big heart and will help anyone before you help yourself. It's very selfless and kind how you care for God's people."

Those words were so encouraging and really excited my spirit. But he Lord spoke to me saying Devon couldn't stay with me. He had to find his own way. I didn't know if I was doing the right thing, and all in honesty, I didn't want to risk what I had been delivered from. I just wanted to be a help. But my God had shown me the right path to walk and I didn't allow Devon to spend the night with me and he left. Besides, Church was about to start in an hour anyway and I needed to focus and prepare for my part. I had been asked to read my poem for the Church Anniversary. The poem, *The 3 T's, Time, Transitioning and Transparency,* I'd be reading, would be giving God's people an overview of how I survived in my most difficult moments, how I overcame, and how I was still standing.

As I wrote, God interrupted me asking. "Do you Trust me?"

"Of course, I do, Lord."

"Take $300 out of that $1,000 you have in the white envelope."

I said, "Yes." I placed the $300 inside my and headed out the door. At the same time, I was praying to God for much strength to face His people. The whole time riding to Church, I was nervous. I still haven't broken out of my shyness.

I got to the Church, and before I knew it, my part was next on the program. *I'm shocked that I'm even standing here about to use my gift of poetry.* As I start to read, all eyes are glued upon me. *I'm sweating as I say every word profoundly.* This is my passion, my talent that God blessed me with. To heal others through my words even in my time of *going through*. It always made my soul rejoice to help others heal while I was healing myself. God sure knows how to help you cope. It is so beautiful how when others receive you receive too!

I absolutely loved it. After I finished reading, everyone applauded. I received a prophetic word standing there. I was pointed out. I was told that I had so much greatness in me. The poems were just the beginning. Keep writing, keep stretching, God is going to use you mightily. You are going somewhere and going to reach out to many. I acknowledged every word with an open heart. Although I'd been called, I was still unsure about what God needed me to do. Church was over, and I received a text message from CJ. She had found me a car for the amount I had, but I needed to give her a few days. She, along with her husband, was trying to work out a payment agreement with the lady who was selling the car. I sent her a text thanking her with all my heart because God was really blessing me. I was so grateful and appreciative at that moment, and God got all the glory.

I found myself becoming very active in the Church and it was nothing God spoke to me about. The assignments came from my pastor, and because I'm so obedient and faithful, I did what I was told. He placed me in charge of the Youth Sunday School. A sense of excitement came over me because I was really big on the youth. I desired to make a difference in their lives, but the assignment, not so much. I also read poems every Sunday or sometimes teach the youth during bible class. I figured I was only told to do this because no one else would deal with Sunday school. That part was always neglected, but I did my part and used my kids every so often to teach, and even my cousin often. Children rarely showed up for Sunday school unless parents were told to bring them. And they barely showed interest when they came. It would get so bad that I would get upset. I spent countless nights losing sleep preparing for Sunday school, and no one showed up. Do you know how discouraging that was to me? I cried out to God and he told me to leave that alone, *Your spirit can't be stuck in one place. You have a traveling spirit.*

What I needed you to do was start a Blog. A BLOG? And I'm thinking, I don't know where to start or how to start. But when God gives you an assignment, and it makes no sense, do it anyhow. I was ministering through Facebook already, so I thought maybe that was enough outreach ministering for me since I had just started. God said, *No I need you to do something else as wel. You know how you use to send out your text messages to everyone in your phone I want you to flip it to your emails sending out daily Touches Monday through Friday.* I was like wow. God is so creative when He wants to get his word out. I wasn't working, or in school, so this was the perfect time to take heed and be about My Father's business. I'm young and on fire for Him. There's no other place I'd rather be than to Serve God and be a Servant to His people.

I'm on the couch in deep thought because now I'm ready to work or go back to school. Ummm or I could do both. Whichever way I was ready to provide and finish what I started. My son is well enough for daycare, so I would check into making arrangements and moves to get things back going. I'm so over sitting in this house doing nothing. I love to move around. I felt stagnant but not so much because I was on a mission for God that kept me busy the majority of the time. I didn't want to rush anything nor get ahead of God, so I stop making plans to simply tell God, "Not my Will but Let your Will be done."

CJ text me saying the lady selling the car, who was also CJ's co-worker wanted $700. Guess who bought her first car the same day PAID-IN-FULL? Me. No more walking, no more asking people for rides, no more giving out gas money, no more worrying CJ, even though she didn't mind. LOL! I could go whenever I needed to go. God is so good I bought my first car without a note, and with my own money and with the help of CJ I'm just like, *Lord what are you up to next, I'm filled with much Joy.*

I didn't waste any time trying to find a job nor sign my kids up for school. I figured God has blessed me with this car to do everything. The time is now to get things back into the rotation. I went to fill out job applications and met with my advisor to sign back up for school. You probably would have thought I've given up by now. NOPE! I didn't care how long it would take, I'm getting my B.S. degree. I worked too hard to let those few classes slip away like that. I don't make excuses. I go. I do until something happens. I have little ones depending on me so there is no way I can stop. I must keep pushing. I went inside to sign up for my courses, we talked, and my advisor always encouraged me to never give, up keep going, have perseverance. Because what matters is finishing the race to walk the stage one day. After taking care of all that, I went to sign both of my kids in daycare, and because the owner saw how faithful I was on my payments, she let one my kids go free, and I paid for the other one. If you don't see the blessings from that $1,070.00 seed I planted, I don't know what you see. I have favor in my life that's continually growing; expanding in ways I never thought could possibly happen.

I'm proud to say I started school and my kids started daycare the next day. I'm glad because I needed this break from them since I rarely had any 'me' time. And if you know me, school is my escape to everything. My mind needed renewing and to be refreshed, and the books would do it for me.

Meanwhile, Devon popped up. This time he ended up spending the night. I could tell something was bothering him by the look on his face. It was clear he had nowhere to go. He needed my help. I knew it was wrong, but I still risked it to only suffer the consequences later. I just knew God was about to get me, but I used the time Devon was there for some relaxation. I fell asleep, and when I woke up, he had cleaned the house, cooked and was attentive to my kids. I had awakened to the smell of some freshly cooked food. I felt like a brand new person. I couldn't remember the last time I had slept like that.

I explained to Devon that I had started school and he seemed excited for me because that's something I always talked his ear off about. I told him how God had spoken to me, telling me to start a blog and do Daily Touches through emailing. He said, "This would be good for you as much as you like to write. This is going to fit you perfectly."

I couldn't agree more. *Here comes this uneasy feeling again.* I knew it was God convicting me. I ignored the feeling and kept talking praying that the feeling would go away.

We had Church, and Devon didn't want to attend. I'm like, "Well dude, you can't stay here. You will have to leave until we make it back. He got mad and stormed out the door. At Church, we were praising God, loving on God, and in the midst of service, my pastor says God told her to tell me to start writing a book about my life. I'm sitting with my mouth wide open. This was confirmation from four years ago. I had already started, which is what you are reading now. But God also enlisted me to write a second book making my poems a daily devotional. Now it all makes sense to me why God told me to start a Blog. I begin to wonder how I will be able to juggle being a single parent, in school and operating full-time in my ministry. Well as you can see. I'm doing it. I DID IT!

Devon sent me a text asking if I had made it home. I hadn't. He insisted that he was going back home for whatever reason. I had no clue, but I thanked him for helping me the time he was there. Part of me didn't want this relationship yet the other part of me did. I was torn. With all I had going on, who would have time for a relationship.but hey, I thought I was superwoman. I had my cape on at all times, every day, trying to be strong for me and everybody else. My plate was full, and I could smell the distractions that were bound to come along with this relationship.

I finally made it home, got us ready for bed, and prepared for a very exciting day ahead of me. I couldn't sleep. I tossed and turned all night. That morning, I went into prayer, asking God to guide me because I thought I was making a mistake. I didn't want to mess up God's plan for me. After prayer, I made sure I had everything I needed for the day. The next thing on my agenda was to drop the kids off at daycare. I made my way to school, circling the parking lot trying to find a park. I ended up finding one close to my building. I walked in the door and my instructor was calling the roll, I didn't hear my name. I sit there confused because I had my schedule in my hand so I know I was in the right class. When I approached her to find out what was going on, she said, "Skyye you've been purged."

Puzzled, I said, "WHAT? How?"

"Did you pay anything for your classes?"

I showed her the receipt where I had paid $1,000 and where the Business Office had set up my payment plan. She told me to go to the Business Office and make sure I showed them what I showed her. I was furious. It was bad enough I had to pay out of pocket. The woman in the office explained to me that I owed them from withdrawing from school for the second or third time. I said, "But no one ran that by me. I was told I didn't have a balance and I asked for my money back."

She said the money I had paid was nonrefundable. "What the hell," came out of my mouth before I knew it. I just cried it out. It was time for my next class and the Lord spoke to me. While I walked, God said, "Go to your car. Don't go back to class. I want you to start over. Go back to Coahoma Community College and sign up for school."

I called my cousin and told her to meet me at her mom's house so she could drive me to Coahoma. She said she had to go that way anyway to finish registering for school. We took my car to save on gas. Riding, laughing, joking, and talking, just having fun, it took us no time to get to Clarksdale. The minute we made it there, I went to the Admissions Office, picked up an application and went to the Social Work department. I asked for Mrs. Done. She was no longer over that department but as I got acquainted with the new lady she pulled up my classes and she said all you have to do is apply for graduation. I'm like *wait, what, let me see.* We both start laughing but she encouraged me to take a few classes along with the one class I needed to boost up my GPA. I agreed and I started the next day. Not only did I do it for me but for my cousin, too. She was having a hard time getting to school. I wanted to help her so she could be and do better for herself also. This was way out of my way but God was blessing me so it was only right that I bless others. So, we rode to school together every day for about two weeks straight, then all of a sudden, my son started getting sick. I knew he wasn't going to get used to the environment no time soon so I had to stop school. But I picked up my son and went right back down there the same day!

This time I talked to Mrs. Done who is like a mother to me. She started out with me in 2009. I was so happy to see her. She had always been beautiful to me and as she smiled at me I embraced it. That made my day so much better. I told her about my situation as tears flowed. I said, "Mrs. Done, all I want to do is graduate."

"You are such a strong person, Skyye, to even come back to finish after all these years," she said. She pulled up my classes, looked at me, and said she was going to get me across that stage in May. "I have an idea," she continued. "I know you want your Degree in Social Work, but you are missing a class. You can get one in General Education and the great part about it you still get you're A.A. Degree and that's all that matters right?"

I hugged her and gave her a big kiss on her jaw. I told her how much I love her and how she always knew what to do and when to do it. She smiled and said my baby will be walking across the stage in May.

"Thank you for not giving up on me," I said.

What we want doesn't always come in the form of what we wish but it's always lined up with God's plan. If I never listens when He speaks, I wouldn't be where I am now. Let the joy of the Lord be your strength. He will see you through as long as you fight and never give up on Him. He will never give up on you.

Can you imagine the smile on my face? I'm so happy I actually got to sit at home chill out until it was graduation time. This gave me so much energy to start on my assignments for God. I was already behind. It's time to play catch up because God's people need me. I took a nap and dreamed:

I was walking on campus at the school. I was also on the phone and a pregnant lady was hit by a car. She was hit so hard she went into labor had the baby right there in the road. She was pushing and hollering because she couldn't stand the unbearable pain. The baby came still born (Dead). God told me to go put my hands around the baby's head. I dropped the phone, started praying and uttering in tongues. The baby came back alive.

The minute I woke up, God spoke right then with no hesitation leaving me no room to wonder. He said, "You hold on to the youth, protect and save them from this cruel world. Teach them about me. Tell them to love me and always keep me first. I need their souls, they need me just as much as the world; the world can't fill the empty voids. Show them the way of forgiveness and repentance."

The joy of hearing from God as He speaks gives my spirit so much hunger. I listen. I obey and take heed to my dreams. This is a way He speaks to me about others, warns me before the destruction comes, and shows me what's about to come to pass all before it happens.

Devon called to apologize. I forgave him and moved forward with the situation. He said he should have stayed because he didn't have anywhere to go. I felt sorry for him and moved him in. We ended up having sex numerous times. I felt bad, I felt sick. I knew this was God whooping me because now I'm shacking with no ring, no commitment, and no husband. Just a live-in boyfriend. And what's funny, I didn't get my ring until after the fact. Can I tell you things were not the same? I ended up with a person I never knew about, a person I never encountered before. This was a whole different man. He had anger issues, he smoked weed, he cursed, he verbally abused me, he never went to Church, he always made excuses, he would leave and stay gone for hours at a time, he didn't want to work. All I'm saying is how was I so blind to this. He used God to get me where he wanted me to be and he dogged me out. He was a distraction to me all along. I didn't pray to God. I mean for what God had been trying to warn me about. So now I have to ride it out and heal the best I know how while I'm trying to get myself back in God. It's hard. I'm repenting, I'm pleading, I'm begging but all I feel is God's wrath. I was dying. Well at least that's what it felt like. I was torn into pieces. I was so lost. I spent many days at the altar confessing, laid out crying my eyes out. All I wanted was to get back to God and never leave Him again.

I will never label Devon as a bad person. He had a lot of bad habits and God really showed me his true colors. When I realized this, I put him out. I threw my ring away and stopped dealing with him. For that moment, I had lost sight of who I was and what I needed. God.

A valuable lesson was learned. I have the time now to help others heal because truth is it was never about me. I'm all for touching lives and hearts. My life is to glorify God so I can get closer to Him. I wanted to work again. I figured I was heads up on everything with my books, my blog, my daily emails. I even started back teaching Sunday school and bible class. I lucked up and found me a temp job that I worked for two weeks. After I caught up on everything, they didn't need me anymore. Plus, I had to wear pants so I ended up leaving that job for good. I acquired another one the same day at my kids daycare doing secretarial work. I had ran out of money, but God made sure my bills were paid. When you take care of Him, He will most certainly take care of you. I worked that job for eight months, and they were the most stressful eight months of my life.

You probably want to know did I continue. No. I actually quit my job to write this book. You are also probably wondering if I graduated. I did. May 14, 2016, and am I married? No, currently waiting on my husband. The pretty lady from the desk, CJ, is still around as well; she is FAMILY. I still have my car. It's been two years now. My son is still a supernatural miracle who is truly a blessing to us all. Because God is head and center, I'm walking into my destiny. I'm here to tell you I MADE IT! Even as a saved woman, life still isn't perfect. I still deal with the challenges that life brings. The difference now, Jesus is here with me. As God showed me about Christian living, my thinking and my actions all changed. I am living a sober life. It is the best thing that could have happened to me. I am a better person, a new woman/role model for my kids. I read and study my bible more. I dress modestly. I even stopped watching TV to be in God's presence. It's a wonderful and beautiful life. I am now a Crowned (JESUS) Butterfly (FREED ME). God has given me the peace in my heart and has changed my life tremendously. He is here every day with me. I hope that while on this journey, you encountered a relationship with God. I hope you have been delivered; I hope you have been healed; and I hope you have been set free. Whatever you can't handle, I encourage you to give it to God because only He can.

My name is Skyye Howze and I'm here to engage with you, encourage you, and enlighten you, but more importantly, draw you closer to God. At your own risk, you can kindly visit my blog. I post every Monday and Wednesday!

The website is below. Because your lives and hearts matter, I will do the honor to heal and help in any way God uses me - God bless you.

http://touchinglives-touchinghearts.my-free.website

If you would like to receive my *Daily Touches* each day, send me an email: skyyehowze@yahoo.com.

Made in the USA
Middletown, DE
20 February 2020